MANIPULATION AND PERSUASION BIBLE

ART OF PERSUASION AND THE BODY LANGUAGE MASTERY ON HUMAN BEHAVIOUR

BY

Craig Cialdini

TABLE OF CONTENT

COPYRIGHT... 23

CHAPTER 1: INTRODUCTION TO BODY LANGUAGE 27

> What is body language? 27

> How does the body speak? 28

> Importance of body language......... 29

> Importance of body language in public speaking 29

> What kind of thing to pay close attention to? 30

> Looking at the crowd..................... 31

> Where are you on stage?................ 31

> Happy vs. sad 31

> Significance of facial gestures: are you laughing? 32

> Types of body language................. 32

> Parts of the body included 33

> Intentions.................................... 35

> Voice tone 36

> Gestures of body language 37

> Postures body language 38

> The body language of movements .. 39

- ➤ Appearance and dressing 40
- ➤ Eyes contact 40
- ➤ Silence 41
- ➤ Modulation of speech 41
- ➤ More examples of body language 42
- ➤ Nail-biting.................................... 42
- ➤ Finger taping or playing drums 43
- ➤ Touching your nose...................... 43
- ➤ The consequence of rubbing your hands... 43
- ➤ Attempting to put fingertips together 43
- ➤ Open hands, face upwards............. 44
- ➤ Head in your hands...................... 44
- ➤ Locking the ankles 44
- ➤ Stroking your cheeks or your mustache...................................... 44
- ➤ Pulling the ear 45
- ➤ Picking of Lint 45
- ➤ Posture of Catapult 46
- ➤ Lower head 46
- ➤ Body language tips 46

- ➢ 1.Assume a power pose to raise your confidence 47
- ➢ 2.To maximum benefit, look like you're listening 48
- ➢ 3.To foster cooperation, eliminate barriers 49
- ➢ 4.Shake hands to communicate directly with others 50
- ➢ 5.Stimulating positive thoughts, smile 51
- ➢ 6.Showing agreement, mirror gestures, and body movements...... 52
- ➢ 7.Using your hands to strengthen your voice... 52
- ➢ 8.Watch people's feet to find the facts 53
- ➢ 9.Keep your voice low to sound definitive 54
- ➢ 10.Uncross your arms and legs to strengthen your memory 54
- ➢ How body language unveils feelings and ideas? 55
- ➢ Why Females are much more observant 56
- ➢ What the brain scans are revealing . 59

➢ The Universal Gesture 61

➢ Three Rules of Successful Reading .. 62

➢ Rule1. Read the Cluster Expressions 62

➢ Law 3. Read Legislation in context . 66

➢ Why children are easier to understand? 68

➢ Can you fake body language? 70

➢ How to Become a Good Reader? 71

➢ How to Detect Transparency? 73

➢ The Five C of the Body Language 75

➢ Filter the first experience 77

CHAPTER 2: MANIPULATION: "TO REGULATE, MANIPULATE OR MANAGE" 89

➢ Manipulation produces an idea of free choice 93

➢ Manipulation is hidden with the target 98

➢ Effects of manipulation on the essential power 101

➢ Persuasion & Hypnotic Effect is almost like learning a foreign language 103

➢ Mental Rehearsal: You should be an actor 103

➢ Get Out of the Comfort Zone........ 104

➢ Start with the objective in mind.... 105

➢ Become a Controller 106

➢ The Controller's Behavior............. 107

➢ Pre-play & Rehearse Performance. 107

➢ Regulation of Anxiety 108

➢ All knowledge is state-dependent . 109

➢ Body Language That Can Make You More Convincing and Pleasant...... 110

➢ The Strength of Body Language to Facilitate Person-to-Person Interactions 111

➢ How to Develop Interpersonal Speech Report and Trust?...................... 113

➢ Act to get the best outcomes spontaneously and genuinely 114

➢ Persuade how to use body language in a convincing argument? 115

➢ For speaking when you stand 117

➢ For speaking while you're sitting down 118

➢ When you speak practically.......... 119

➢ Observe the body language of the crowd................................... 121

CHAPTER 3: USE OF BODY LANGUAGE FOR PERSUADING 124

- The eyes do not deceptive 125
- Show Commitment and Passion by Hand Gestures 128
- Always sure that your facial expression matches your speech .. 130
- Assume the rooted role of the Express Trust................................... 130
- How to persuade people by using psychological theories?............... 131
- 1)Hypothesis of Enhancement 132
- 2)Theory of conversion 132
- 3)Theory of Intelligence Processing 132
- 4)Priming up 133
- 5)Reciprocity norm 134
- 6)Principle of availability 134
- 7)Sleeper Consequences 134

> 8)External effects 135

> 9)Change in Yale Mentality Approach 135

> 10)Absolute terms and conditions 136

> 7 Forms Compelling Body Gestures Reinforce Company Presentations . 136

> Arrange your pose like a Superman 137

> Stand up straight........................ 138

> Open up your muscles................. 139

> Take a look in the eyes of the audience 139

> Move around comfortably 140

> Use your hands 141

> Relax the facial muscles 141

CHAPTER 4: STRATEGIC INTERPRETATION OF BODY LANGUAGE 144

> The shake of the shoulder is a familiar gesture not to know what's going on 145

> Open palms are a typical example of authenticity 146

➢ A pointing finger with a closed hand is an attempt to assert superiority ... 146

➢ Check for lack of wrinkles around the eyes to spot a false expression 147

➢ Raised eyebrows are also indicators of distress 148

➢ They're probably concerned if their voice goes up or down................. 148

➢ If they mimic the language of your body, the conversation is generally going well 149

➢ Eye contact indicates curiosity, both positive and negative 149

➢ But if they've been staring into your eyes for so long, they may be cheating 150

➢ Extensive posture signals strength and a feeling of accomplishment........ 150

➢ Crossed legs are typically a symbol of reluctance and low receptivity, which are a negative sign of bargaining.. 151

➢ A 'cluster' of movements reveals a strong sense of interaction.......... 151

➢ Whether they laugh at you, they're definitely into you 151

➤ A clenched jaw, a clenched neck, or a furrowed forehead indicates tension 152

➤ Expansive, influential positions demonstrate leadership 153

➤ A trembling leg signifies an unstable inner state 153

➤ Crossed weapons can indicate defensiveness, depending on the context 154

➤ Persuasive body language positions 154

➤ The box position (trustworthy) 155

➤ To hold a ball (Dominant, commanding)............................. 155

➤ Pyramid-hands (relaxes, self-confidence)................................ 156

➤ Wide stance (in control, confident) 156

➤ Palms up (accepting, honest) 157

➤ Palms down (emphatic, strong) 157

➤ Proven Convincing Strategies 157

➤ Use your hands during a speech ... 158

➤ Be a Wordsmith.......................... 160

➤ Tap the sensory experiences 162

➤ Storytelling presentation 163

➢ Use the Sensitivity to Failure 163

➢ Be polite 164

➢ "Beats" (or "Rhythmic Gesture") ... 167

➢ "Points" (or "textual expressions") 168

➢ "The Designs" (or the Iconic Gestures) 169

➢ "Metaphors" (or Analog Gestures) . 170

➢ "Placeholders" (or Unified Gesture) 170

CHAPTER 5: SIGNIFICANCE OF BODY LANGUAGE IN PUBLIC DISCOURSE 174

➢ The Empathy Theory 176

➢ Why Physical Action Support? 177

➢ 01.Messages are more unforgettable than that 177

➢ 02.Punctuation gives value to it 179

➢ 03.Nervous Stress transformed 180

➢ Five ways of making Your Body Talk Powerful 181

➢ I.Eliminate the Distractive Mannerisms 182

➢ II.Be Normal, Informal, Conversational 185

➢ III.Let your body look at your emotions 185

➢ IV.Gain self-confidence through preparedness 186

➢ V.Use your club as a laboratory for learning 187

➢ You're Speech Style 188

➢ Expressions 190

➢ Why Gestures? 193

➢ Gesture Categories 194

➢ How to Treat Efficiently? 197

➢ 1. React to, of course, what you hear, feel, and tell 197

➢ 2. Establish the conditions of management 198

➢ 3. Follow the term action and the occasion 199

➢ 4. Keep Your Actions Compelling .. 201

➢ 5. Make the movements quick and time-consuming 202

➢ 6. Make natural, natural gesturing a habit 203

➢ Body movements 204

➢ Facial Movement 208

➢ Eye contact...................................... 212

➢ Why is communication with the eye essential? 212

➢ How to use your eyes efficiently ... 216

➢ Visual input control 218

➢ How to make the first impression? 220

➢ Appearance matters a lot............. 221

➢ When you speak to the audience .. 223

➢ The first-minute importance 224

➢ Thumbs up on expressions........... 225

CHAPTER 6: ROUTES TO THE CONVINCING, CORE, AND PERIPHERAL 227

➢ Primary Route 229

➢ Peripheral route........................... 230

➢ Determinants of progress 232

➢ Elaboration implications............... 233

➢ Several functions 235

➢ How better you react to body language ....?235

CHAPTER 7: ART OF PERSUASION 248

➢ Is persuasion an art, and why?..... 249

➢ What is the point of persuasiveness? 250

➢ Factors to be considered in the art of convincing 251

➢ How to Practice Persuasiveness? .. 255

➢ Get the Appropriate Introduction .. 255

➢ Worth of the hearing 256

➢ When you don't believe, be respectful 257

➢ Subtlety is essential 258

➢ Persuasion and Values 258

➢ Whose opinion matters? 259

➢ Legal issues 260

➢ Undue interference 260

➢ Misrepresenting statements 261

➢ Perpetual Scams......................... 261

➢ Is convincing positive or negative? 262

➢ Secrets of persuasive people........ 263

➢ 1.They know about their audience 264

➢ 2.They connect with the audience 264

➢ 3.They don't push others 265

➢ 4.They're not the mousy 266

- ➢ 5.Using constructive body language 267
- ➢ 6.They are both straightforward and precise 267
- ➢ 7.They are real and honest 268
- ➢ 8.They consider your point of view 269
- ➢ 9.They ask good questions 270
- ➢ 10.Visual presentations 271
- ➢ 11.They leave a positive first impression 271
- ➢ 12.They know how to stand in front of audiences 272
- ➢ 13.They recognize people by name 273
- ➢ 14.They are pleasers 274
- ➢ 15.They always keep smiling 274
- ➢ How to read and persuade people with six robust courtroom techniques? . 275
- ➢ Recognize the 'three personality positions' 275

- ➢ Understand and sympathize 276
- ➢ Be honest 277
- ➢ Focus on body language and voice tone 278
- ➢ Address your objections 279
- ➢ Principles of persuasion 280
- ➢ 1.Persuasion is not manipulation 280
- ➢ 2.Convince the Persuadable 280
- ➢ 3.Timing and Context 281
- ➢ 4.You've to be involved in being convinced 282
- ➢ 5.Cooperation obligates 282
- ➢ 6.The Consistency in a work 283
- ➢ 7.Perfectly complement 283
- ➢ 8.Place your objectives 284
- ➢ 9.Don't presume 284

➢ 10. Build your scarcity 285

➢ 11. Build Emergency 285

➢ 12. Graphics matters a lot 286

➢ 13. Tell the truth 286

➢ 14. Develop a relationship 287

➢ 15. Flexibility of actions 287

➢ 16. Learn how to pass energy 288

➢ 17. Communicate clearly and effectively 288

➢ 18. Being organized give you the edge 289

➢ 19. Keep calm and isolate in confrontation 289

➢ 20. Use frustration for intent 290

➢ 21. Conviction and self-assurance 290

➢ Psychological convincing strategies 291

➢ Main Persuasion Strategies 292

➢ Trying to create a need 292

➢ Adjust to societal needs 293

➢ Use words and pictures 294

➢ Put your foot on the doorstep....... 294

➢ Go large, then little.................... 295

➢ Use the force of mutual support ... 296

➢ Establish an anchor point for your corporation 297

➢ Limit the availability................... 297

➢ Spend time notifying convincing communications 298

➢ How to detect emotions, deceit, and distress?................................. 299

➢ What Breathing and skin alteration means? 300

➢ Shaking body 302

➢ Shaking of muscles.................... 304

➢ What the eyes can reveal?........... 305

➢ How people show self-soothing habits? 306

➢ Eye contact is a prove to truth 308

➢ The response of mouth and lips.... 309

➢ Involuntary muscles action 310

➢ Deliberately misleading talk 311

CHAPTER 8: BODY LANGUAGE MASTERY 315

➢ Get some encouragement 316

➢ Strengthen your body language for your reading skills 316

➢ Convey body language to others... 317

➢ Remove micro-expressions 318

➢ Understand ethical values 318

➢ Non-verbal regulatory skills 319

➢ Different ways constructive body language will make your life a better one 319

➢ 1.Change the behavior 320

➢ 2.Enhance the presence 321

➢ 3.Tends to increase testosterone 321

➢ 4.Prevent confrontation 322

➢ 5.Talk better to people 322

➢ 6.Decreases the stress hormone 323

➤ 7.Improves emotional, intellectual ability 323

➤ Unusual facts about body language reading 324

➤ It's not all black and white 325

➤ Facial body language can be tricky to read................................... 326

➤ Body language indicates the purpose 327

➤ Read the body language of the people you know 328

➤ Body movements hack to control frustration and other aggressive emotion.................................... 328

➤ Lookup...................................... 329

➤ Keep smiling 330

➤ Take a deep breath..................... 331

➤ Write it down 332

➤ How to use nonverbal communication to improve the mood? 333

➤ Move and free up your mind 334

➤ Force a smile to raise the mood.... 335

➤ Trying to dance to stay positive.... 335

CONCLUSION 338

COPYRIGHT............................... 342

COPYRIGHT

©Copyright 2020 by "Craig Cialdini"

All rights reserved

This book:

"Manipulation and Persuasion bible: Art of Persuasion and the Body Language Mastery on Human Behavior."

Written By

Craig Cialdini

This document aims to provide precise and reliable details on this subject and the problem under discussion.

A statement of principle is a subcommittee of the American Bar Association, a committee of publishers, and is approved. A copy, reproduction, or distribution of parts of this text, in electronic or written form, is not permitted.

The recording of this document is strictly prohibited. Any retention of this text is only with the written permission of the publisher and all liberties authorized.

The information provided here is correct and reliable, as any lack of attention or other means resulting from the misuse or use of the procedures or instructions contained therein is the total, and absolute obligation of the user addressed.

The author is not obliged, directly or indirectly, to assume civil liability for any restoration, damage, or loss resulting from the data collected here. The respective authors retain all copyrights not kept by the publisher.

The information contained herein is solely and universally available for information purposes. The data is presented without a warranty or promise of any kind.

The trademarks used are without approval, and the patent is issued without the trademark owner's permission or protection.

The logos and labels in this book are the property of the owners themselves and are not associated with this text.

CHAPTER 1: INTRODUCTION TO BODY LANGUAGE

What is body language?

Body language is a non-verbal expression that includes body activity. "Operation" may also be referred to as body language, an entirely non-verbal means of communication. People in the office can share a great deal of knowledge without speaking; by non-verbal contact. Not all of our principles, opinions, feelings, and goals are orally expressed. Any of these are conveyed non-verbally in the current conversation. In Non-verbal communication, our human body communicates our thoughts and actions through conscious and unconscious emotions and postures, followed by gestures, facial expressions, eye contact, and touch. Collectively, this forms a distinct vocabulary of the body within the context of an active conversation. It's called Body Language.

How does the body speak?

Our human body communicates through conscious and unconscious emotions and actions, hand gestures, facial expressions, eye movements, and contact. Any of these bodily motions of the body parts may be used as individual terms and could be understood differently by other human beings within a specific framework of contact.

Importance of body language

Since perceptions of body language vary from people to people and cultures in different countries, it is interesting to learn about them. The body language alone is 55% of the overall speech, while the spoken word is 7%, and the voice tone is 38%.

Importance of body language in public speaking

Why is body language so important? You may tell that having the wrong body language means that your talk will hardly be a victory. You need a lot of talent for other things to make up for poor body language. Examples of poor body language include: turning your back to the crowd, jumping around too often, or standing behind a table. Effective management may harm your speaking, also. Becoming overly loud in your movements, drumming your fingers, or even chewing your nails is poor examples. But even if you're not doing a bad job, improving your body's language can significantly impact. The audience receives your speaking, particularly on the way. It can make a distinction between chatting politely and persuading people. That's why everyone needs to pay attention to that.

What kind of thing to pay close attention to?

Better body language means that you pay attention to various things. For example, you need to know how to walk, where to look, where to stay, and what movements to make.

Looking at the crowd

Are you looking at your audience? Or are you one of those commentators who prefer to gaze at the screen behind you? Are you paying attention to your whole audience and not just a few lucky ones?

Where are you on stage?

As a presenter, you need to know where you're on track. It means you've got to think about where you're going to go in a group debate and whether to (not) move around.

Happy vs. sad

What idea are you going to get through with your body? Are you displaying your happiness? Why are you upset about that? This is focusing on the viewers.

Significance of facial gestures: are you laughing?

Did you know, for example, that smiling makes people more relaxed as a speaker with you? In public speaking, facial expressions are highly significant. The way you smile says a lot about how you feel and your speech. At the same time, you don't want to be laughing at a sad story. Your facial expressions should be in line with your narrative.

Types of body language

What kinds of body language can be differentiated?

The body language is generally separated into two parts.

1. Parts of the body

2. Purpose of creating

So, what styles can be included in each category of people?

Parts of the body included

From head to foot, here are classes for body parts:

- Head-Movement and turning of the head, front to back, right to left, side to side, including tossing the heads.
- The facial gestures-The face has several muscles (anywhere between 54 and 98, depending on who you ask) that move many parts of the face. Every variation of gestures of

the following facial elements expresses the state of mind:

- Eyebrows, raised, down, scowling.
- Eyes-Left, right, up, down, grinning, eye tapping.
- Nose-Wrinkle (at the top) and twitching of the nostrils.
- Lips-Smiling, snarling, puckering, licking, opening, closing.
- Tongue-In, back, flipped, tip-up or down, licking the lips.
- Mouth-Open, locked, clinked, lower jaw left, or right.
- Body Posture-The way you position your body and arms and legs in comparison to each other and someone else:
- Body proximity-How far or near to someone.
- The motions of the shoulder-up, down, standing, hunched.

- Positioning of arms-up, down, bent, upright.
- The positioning of legs and knees-straight, bent, placing of weight, knees against a talking partner or pointing somewhere, slipping feet.
- Hand and finger gestures-The way you handle and move your hands and fingers is exceptionally informative in the reading of people.
- Handling and positioning of items (e.g., markers, documents, etc.). -The weird one out of here. Technically not a body part, but objects play a significant role in body language interpretation.

Intentions

Another way to organize the forms of body language is by Intent:

- Voluntary / Intentional motions-usually referred to as "expressions." These are the gestures you were trying to make, like raising a hand, offering a finger, blinking with one eye.

- Repetitive movements-usually referred to as "tells," but "ticks" often fall under this group. Anybody activity you don't have any control overcomes in this range. Although there is theoretically no movement of the muscle, sweating still appears.

Voice tone

Though generally used as body language, the tone of voice and pronunciation is different from the body language.

For the sake of completeness, below are the classes that can be contained in the tone of voice:

- Voice pitch-high, medium voice, intonation.
- Loudness-Everything from yelling to moaning.
- Breathing-Slow, rapid breathing, shaky voice.

Gestures of body language

"It is the expressive movements of a part of the body, particularly of the hands or heads."

- It has a critical impact as a component of oral speech.
- A person's expression conveys much more than he says.
- The wave of a hand to signify goodbye or to attract a person's attention.

- Shaking hands are demonstrating affection.
- Shrugging of the shoulders shows ignorance and unconcern.
- The index finger shows an accusation or claim.
- The thumbs-up symbol shows that you like "Good Luck."

Postures body language

- Means "the body's behavior or position."
- Each action of the body has expressive and protective functions.
- The way we sit, stand, and walk out shows us a lot about ourselves.
- Well, a strong stance shows a positive attitude.

The body language of movements
Expression of the face

- All facial organs on the human face suggest a descriptive facial message.
- Hair, forehead, eyebrows, eyes, chest, jaw, nose, neck, ears, teeth, tongue, etc.
- Facial gestures come spontaneously and are thus beyond the influence of the speaker.

Examples of facial gestures

- The expression reflects love and appreciation.
- The lifted eyebrows express surprises.
- A furrowed brow reflects concern and fear.
- Frown indicates annoyance or mistrust.

Appearance and dressing

- The type of dress we wear and the way we style ourselves to demonstrate our value and mood.
- We've affected how others pose and what they wear.
- Physical appearance plays a significant part in our perception of individuals.
- People's clothing and personal appearance express a lot of details about them.

Eyes contact

- Eye contact has a lot to do with face-to-face conversation.
- Lack of eye contact indicates a loss of confidence and comprehension.
- We look more quickly rather than listening or communicating.
- The eyes are human portals, except that there is no existence.

- The speaker would look in the audience's eyes from right to left and from left to right, building confidence and reducing nervousness.
- Construct the relationship between the speaker and the audience.

Silence

- "Talking is silver, but silence is gold."
- It points out the relationship between the communicators.
- Moments of silence – You don't know how to keep going.

Modulation of speech

- The speaker must make fair use of his voice.
- Someone needs to be a successful speaker; a strong speaker is a must.
- A strong voice is a blessing of God.

- One should take phonetics lessons to develop one's voice.

More examples of body language

Arms folded in front of the chest. This is one of the instances of body language that shows that one is defensive. The body language indicating crossed arms can often indicate dissatisfaction with the views and actions of other people with whom you speak.

Nail-biting

This example of body language suggests that one is lost in thinking, possibly thinking something. You can be in deep focus while your hand is on your cheek, and your brows are furrowed.

Finger taping or playing drums

This behavior reveals that while waiting, one is growing strained or anxious.

Touching your nose

Touching or scratching your nose means indifference, dismissal, or lying about something.

The consequence of rubbing your hands

This may indicate that your hands are cold, which may mean that you're anxious about something, or you're ready to wait.

Attempting to put fingertips together

This is called "steepling" or bringing fingertips together to show power or authority.

Open hands, face upwards

The gesture is a symbol of integrity, loyalty, and innocence. This is how some people show respect and obedience.

Head in your hands

The body language of this expression may be one of frustration, be angry, or be embarrassed because you don't want to expose your face.

Locking the ankles

When you're seated or standing, while your ankles are closed, you express anxiety or nervousness.

Stroking your cheeks or your mustache

This expresses when one is immersed in thought. This behavior is always performed unintentionally as one attempts to come up with a decision.

Pulling the ear

Pulling an ear lobe may mean that you're trying to make a choice, but you're always indecisive about anything.

Picking of Lint

Catching an imagined lint is another example of the body language of displacement movements, which one uses to demonstrate criticism of the actions or views of others. This gesture lets one turn away from the other when performing some meaningless gesture.

Posture of Catapult

This seated version of the "Hand-on-Hip" male poster, with the hands behind the head and the elbows sticking out, is used to threaten or show a relaxed attitude. This provides a false sense of protection before an attempt is made.

Lower head

This means that one of us is hiding something. You may display shyness, embarrassment, or timidity when you lower your head when you are praised. It can also express that you keep a distance from another person, show skepticism, or think about yourself.

Body language tips

The healthy language of the body may be trained. You will do this by rehearsing or preparing in front of your peers. You must be vigilant of the training in front of the Mirror. The rugged use of body language plays a vital role in the conversation. Many of our verbal training courses have an element of body language to them. Here are ten tips for functional body language that we've learned from coaching teams worldwide over the past two decades.

1. Assume a power pose to raise your confidence

Study at Harvard, and Columbia Business Schools demonstrates that merely keeping the body in spacious, "high-powered" positions (leaning back with the hands behind your head and feet up on your desk, or standing with your legs and arms widely open) for as little as two minutes induces higher levels of testosterone. A hormone-related to strength and dominance and lower levels of cortisol, a stress hormone. Try this when you are threatened. However, you want to be confident. In addition to triggering behavioral changes in both males and females, these poses contribute to increased feelings of dominance and enhanced risk perception. The study also showed that people are more frequently affected by how they feel about you than what you think.

2. To maximum benefit, look like you're listening

If you want people to strike up a conversation, don't think about multitasking when chatting. Avoid the temptation to check your text messages, check your watch, or check how the other participants respond. Instead, concentrate on those who speak by rotating the head and body to face them squarely and making eye contact.

Bending forward, smiling, and tilting your head are other non-verbal ways that indicate you're involved and paying attention. It's essential to understand people. It's almost as necessary to make sure they know that you're listening.

3. To foster cooperation, eliminate barriers

Physical obstructions are incredibly harmful to cooperative efforts. Take out something that blocks your vision or establishes a bridge between you and the rest of the team. Particularly after a coffee break, be mindful that you can create a shield by keeping your cup and saucer in a way that appears to obstruct your body or pull you hidden from others purposely. A senior executive told me that he could measure the satisfaction of his colleagues from how high they kept their cups of coffee. It was his finding that the most dangerous situations they saw, the higher they kept their coffee. People with their hands held at the waist level felt more relaxed than those with high shoulders.

4. Shake hands to communicate directly with others

Touch is the most basic and robust non-verbal cue. Touch others on the arm, hand, or shoulder for as little as 1/40 of a second establishes a social connection. Physical touch and warmth are created in the office by a handshaking practice, and this physical interaction provides a permanent and optimistic feeling. Handshake research by the Income Center for Trade Shows found that people are twice as likely to recognize you if you shake hands with them. Researchers also observed that people respond to those they shake hands by being more open and welcoming.

5. Stimulating positive thoughts, smile

A real smile not only improves your sense of well-being; it also shows everyone around you that you are approachable, friendly, and honest. A genuine expression gently comes out, crisscrosses the eyes, lights up the face, and eventually fades away. Most notably, smiling impacts explicitly how other people react to you. When you smile at others, they're almost always smiling in return. And, since facial gestures evoke similar emotions, the smile you get back really affects the mental state of the person positively.

6. Showing agreement, mirror gestures, and body movements

If customers or company partners unwittingly mimic your body language, it's their way of non-verbally saying that they like or agree with you. If you imitate other people intently, it can be an essential aspect of establishing relationships and developing feelings of mutuality. Mirroring begins by watching a person's face and body movements and then consciously making the body take on identical expressions and postures. Doing this would make the other person feel appreciated and accepted.

7. Using your hands to strengthen your voice

Brain Imaging has shown that a region called the Broca field, which is critical for speech development, is activated not only when we speak, but when we wave our hands. As the action is integrally connected to the voice, behaving when we say it will potentially enhance our thoughts.

8. Watch people's feet to find the facts

When people want to regulate their body language, they rely mostly on facial expressions, body postures, and hand/arm movements. Although the knees and the thighs are left hidden, they are often where the reality can most frequently be found. Under pressure, people also demonstrate nervousness and discomfort by increased foot movements. Feet are going to fidget, move, and wind around each other or the chairs. Feet rolls and twists to alleviate stress, or even kicks off in a miniaturized effort to escape free.

9. Keep your voice low to sound definitive

During a speech or a significant phone call, encourage the voice to calm at its highest pitch through holding the lips close and creating "um hum, hem hum, hem hum" sounds. And if you're a woman, note sure your voice doesn't raise at the end of the sentence as though you were posing a query or requesting permission. Instead, when you express your opinion, use the authoritative arc, where the voice begins on one line, increases in pitch through the phrase, then drops back down at the end.

10. Uncross your arms and legs to strengthen your memory

Body Language Researchers share an interesting finding from one of their studies. When a team of enthusiasts attended a lecture and sat with their arms and legs extended, they recalled 38% better than the community who participated and sat with their arms and legs folded. Uncross your arms and legs to boost your persistence. If you see the crowd showing aggressive body language, change tactics, take a rest, or ask them to move — and don't attempt to force them before their bodies open up.

If you follow these ten essential and useful body language tips, I guarantee that you can maximize your non-verbal effect on the workplace. To develop your leadership skills as a whole, try taking a course in communications.

How body language unveils feelings and ideas?

Body language is an implicit expression of the mental state of an individual. An action or word may be a valuable link to a person's emotion at that moment. For example, a man who is self-conscious about increasing weight may tug at the fold of the skin under his chin; a woman who is mindful of extra pounds on her thighs may loosen her dress; a female who feels nervous or insecure may fold her arms or cross her legs or both. The trick to interpreting body language can understand it. The mental state of a person when listening to what they are saying and mentioning the conditions in which they were you claim it. This helps you to distinguish reality from fantasy and fiction. In current years, humans have obsessed with the spoken word and our desire to be a conversationalist. Many citizens, however, are surprisingly ignorant of this.

Why Females are much more observant
When telling someone's 'perceptive' or 'sensitive' about others, we're unknowingly

referring to their capacity to interpret the body language of another person and compare these signs with verbal signals. In other words, when we say that we have a 'hunk' or 'good feeling' that someone has told us a lie, we generally mean that their body language and their spoken words don't match. This is also what speakers call collective consciousness or group awareness. For, e.g., if the crowd is seated back in their chairs with their chins down and their arms crossed over their chest, a 'perceptive' speaker would get a hunch or sense that his speech was not going well.

He would understand that he wanted to take a new path to reach the crowd. Likewise, a speaker who wasn't 'perceptive' would have blundered. Overall, women are much more discerning than men, which has led to what is widely referred to as 'women's intuition.' Women have an inherent capacity to pick up and interpret non-verbal messages and a keen eye for specific information. That's why few husbands can lie to their wives and get away with it, and why, on the other hand, most women can pull the wool over the eyes of a man without considering it. A study by psychologists has found that women are much more attentive to body language than men. They displayed short scenes, with the sound switched off, of a man and a woman talking, and the participants were asked to interpret what was going on by analyzing the faces of the people. Analysis has found that women interpret the condition, precisely 87% of the time, while men are just 42% efficient.

Men in 'nurturing' professions, such as musical forms, acting, and nursing, did about the same thing as women; gay men even scored high. Women's intuition is especially apparent in people who have raised children. For the first few years, the mother depends nearly entirely on the non-verbal contact medium with the kid. This is why women are always more perceptive negotiators than men since they practice early reading of signs.

What the brain scans are revealing

Many people have a brain structure to connect to every man on the planet. Magnetic Resonance Imaging brain scans (MRIs) specifically demonstrate that women have a much better able to interact with and assess people than men do. Women have between 14 and 16 regions of the brain to determine the actions of others over the individual in four to six areas. This illustrates how a woman will attend a dinner party and easily hear about the friendship of other partners at the table who has argued. It also illustrates why, from a woman's point of view, men don't seem to speak much, and, from a man's point of view, women never want to shut up.

The female brain is designed for multitasking — the average woman will juggle between two and four different subjects simultaneously. She will watch a TV show while chatting on the phone, then listen to a second chat behind her while drinking a cup of coffee. In one discussion, she will speak about multiple subjects and use five-voice tones to shift the issue or highlight points. Unfortunately, only three of these tones can be identified by most persons. As a result, men frequently lose their focus as women attempt to interact with them. Studies suggest that a person who depends on clear visual evidence face to face about the actions of another person is more likely to make more informed decisions about another person than someone who relies solely on their gut feelings. The proof is in the person's body language, and while women can do it consciously or unconsciously, everyone should train themselves to interpret the signs consciously. That's precisely what this book is about.

The Universal Gesture

The shoulder shrug is also a clear example of a common expression used to indicate that a person does not know or understand what you mean. It is multiple gestures with three main parts: open palms to show that nothing is hidden in the hands, hunched shoulders to shield the neck from attack, and raised brow, a standard, promiscuous greeting. Just as verbal language varies from culture to culture, confident body language signs can also vary. Whereas one gesture may be familiar in a specific culture and may have a simple sense, it may be irrelevant in another culture or may have a different significance.

Three Rules of Successful Reading

What you see and hear in some situations does not generally reflect the actual behaviors that people may have. You need to obey three simple principles to get it right.

Rule1. Read the Cluster Expressions

One of the most significant faults that a beginner can make in body language is interpreting a single gesture in isolation from other movements or situations. For example, scratching your head can mean a variety of things – sweating, confusion, dandruff, fleas, forgetfulness, or deception – depending on the various movements that coincide. As every spoken language, body language includes vocabulary, phrases, and punctuation. The gesture is like a single word, and an available name may have many different meanings. For, e.g., in English, the term 'dressing' has at least ten implications, including the process of putting on clothes, the sauce for food, the stuffing for a chicken, the application for a cut, the fertilizer, and the grooming for a horse. It's when you place a word in a conversation of other words that you can completely understand its meaning. Gestures arrive in 'sentences' called clusters, which inevitably show the collections.

A body language cluster, much like a verbal sentence, has at least three words in it before each word can be clearly described. The 'perceptive' person is the one who can read body language sentences and balance them precisely to the person's verbal corrections. So often look at the clusters of movements for an accurate interpretation. - Each of us has repeated signs that indicate that we're either bored or under pressure. Continual hair touching or twirling is a typical indication of this. However, in contrast to other movements, it is likely to indicate that the individual is insecure or nervous. People stroke their hair or head because that's how their mother comforted them when they were young.

To prove the argument regarding clusters, here is a typical the most Important Appraisal symbol is the hand-to-face gesture, with the index finger pointing up the cheek while the other finger is shielding the mouth and the thumb safeguarding the chin. Further confirmation that this person has severe feelings for what he sees is that the legs are near crossed, and the arm covers the body (defensive) while the head and the chin are down (negative/hostile). This body language 'sentence' means things like, 'I don't like what you're doing,' 'I disagree,' or 'I hold back bad emotions.'

Research indicates that non-verbal signals have about five times as much effect as verbal signals. When the two are incongruous, people, particularly women, rely on non-verbal messages and neglect oral information. If you as the speaker, were to ask the listener mentioned above to give his opinion about what you said, and he responded that he disagreed with you, his body language gestures would be compatible with his verbal statements. That is, they would fit. If he was to say that he agreed with what you said, he would be more inclined to lie because his vocabulary and actions would occur incongruously. If you see a politician standing behind a rostrum speaking proudly but with his arms near crossed over his chest (defensive). And head down (critical/hostile) while reminding his crowd how welcoming and open he is too young people's thoughts; would you be convinced? What if he wanted to reassure you of his warm, loving attitude when giving the lectern short, fast karate chops? Observation of the clusters of gestures and the compatibility of the verbal and body language sources are the keys to a detailed understanding of attitudes by body language.

Law 3. Read Legislation in context

The context in which they occur, all movements should be considered. For example, if someone was seated at the bus terminal with his arms and legs near crossed and head down, and it was a cold winter's day, that would most definitely mean he was freezing, not defensive. If the person used the same expressions when sitting across the table attempting to sell him a concept, product, or service, that may be accurately interpreted as implying that the person was feeling pessimistic or refusing the proposal. Throughout this book, all body language movements will be viewed in context, and, where possible, the clusters of actions will be analyzed. Why it may be simple to misread?

Everyone who has a soft or sloppy handshake — especially a man who is likely to be suspected of being frail. But if anyone has arthritis in their hands, they're more probably to use a gentle handshake to prevent the agony of a firm one. Likewise, artists, singers, surgeons, and others whose work is fragile and require their hands usually tend not to shake hands, although, if they are coerced into it, they can use a 'dead fish' handshake to shield their hands.

Someone who wears inappropriate or tight clothes may not be able to use such gestures, which may influence their use of body language. For example, obese people cannot cross their legs. Women wearing short skirts will sit with their legs near crossed for safety, but this will make them look less open and less likely to be invited to dance in the nightclub. These conditions apply to a minority of individuals, but it is essential to recognize the effects that physical limitations or disabilities may have on the mobility of an individual.

Why children are easier to understand?
Older people are challenging to read than younger people, and they have less muscle tone in their mouths. The pace of specific movements, and how clear they appear to others, is often connected to the age of the person. For, e.g., if a five-year-old boy says

a lie, he's likely to instinctively cover his mouth with one or both of his hands. The act of shielding the mouth will warn the parent to the falsehood, and this mouth-covering action is likely to occur for the life of the child, typically only differing in the pace at which it is performed. When a teenager says a lie, the hand is taken to the mouth in the same manner as a five-year-old. Except in the simple hand-slapping gesture above the mouth, the fingertips rub softly across it. In adulthood, the initial mouth-covering action becomes much more comfortable. When an adult says a lie, it's as if his brain instructs his hand to shield his mouth to hide the dishonest words, just as he did with the five-year-old and the teenager. But, at the last minute, the hand is drawn away from the mouth, and a nose-touch gesture is made. It's also the adult version of the mouth-covering motion that was used in childhood. This illustrates how, as people grow older, their movements get more involved and less noticeable, and that's why it's sometimes more challenging to understand the actions of a fifty-year-old than those of a five-year-old.

Can you fake body language?

We're asked daily, 'Can you have fake body language? 'The general response to this question is 'no' because of the lack of unity that is likely to exist between the significant movements, the micro-signals of the body, and the spoken words. For e.g., open palms are synonymous with sincerity, but when the faker holds out his hands and smiles at you as he tells a lie, his micro-gestures give him away. His eyes will widen, one eyebrow will raise, or the corner of his mouth will twitch, and these signs counter the open hand expression and the genuine smile. As a consequence, receivers, particularly women, tend not to believe what they hear.

How to Become a Good Reader?

Set aside at least 15 minutes a day to research the body language of other people and become conscious of your movements. A firm reading ground is where people meet and connect. The airport is a mostly right place to experience the full continuum of human expressions. People freely communicate their eagerness, rage, sadness, pleasure, impatience, and many other emotions by body language. Group events, corporate meetings, and gatherings are similarly fantastic. Television also provides a great way to read. Switch the volume off and try to visualize what's going on by seeing the image first. By turning the volume on every few minutes, you'll be able to check how correct your non-verbal readings are, and, before long, you'll be able to see the whole show without any volume and understand what's going on, just as deaf people do.

Learn to interpret body language cues not only make you more consciously aware of how others are trying to control and exploit. It helps you understand that others are sometimes doing the same thing to us, and, most critically, it allows us to be more open to other people's thoughts and emotions. We also observed the rise of a new type of social scientist-the Body Language Watcher. Even as a bird watcher likes to keep birds and their actions, so the Body Language Watcher delights in observing the non-verbal signs and gestures of human beings. He watches them at social events, on the beaches, on tv, in the workplace, or wherever people communicate. He is a relational student who needs to learn about the behaviors of his fellow people so that he can potentially learn more about himself and how he can strengthen his interaction with others.

How to Detect Transparency?

If people try to be vulnerable or honest, they always hold one or both palms out to the other person and say something like, 'I didn't do that! I'm sorry if I offended you,' or 'I told you the truth.' If anyone tries to open up or be honest, they are likely to show any or half of their palms to the other person. As other body language gestures, this is an implicit expression that gives you a 'natural' impression or a hunch that the other person tells. When children lie or try hiding something, they frequently cover their hands behind their backs.

Similarly, a man who wants to cover his whereabouts after a night out with the boys may hide his hands in his pockets, or an arm-crossed pose, explaining to his wife where he was. But hidden palms can give her an innate feeling that she's not telling the truth. A woman who is trying to hide something will try to avoid a topic or chat about a variety of unrelated issues while doing different other activities at the same time. Salespeople are trained to watch the customer's uncovered palms as they give excuses or protests as to why they can't purchase a commodity. When anyone offers legitimate reasons, they usually reveal their hands. When people are open to justify their reasoning, they use their hands and show their eyes, when someone who isn't telling the truth is likely to give the same verbal explanations, just to hide their hands. Holding their hands in their pockets is a favorite item of men who don't want to take part in a conversation. Initially, the palms were like the vocal cords in body language, so they were more 'talking' than any other body part, and holding them away was like having one's mouth shut.

The Five C of the Body Language

Body language is like a machine. We all know what it is, but most of us never know precisely how it operates. That's because the method of obtaining and transmitting non-verbal messages is always performed without our conscious consideration. Human beings are genetically designed to check for signals of facial and actions and to grasp their significance rapidly. We see a gesture from another, and we immediately judge the purpose of that motion. And we've been doing it for a long, long time. As humans, we learned how to acquire friends and influence people — or avoid those we couldn't be friends with — long before we understood how to use expressions. Our ancestors took survival choices based entirely on the complex pieces of visual knowledge they obtained from others. There is a world of knowledge that you can discover about people by actually watching how they use their bodies to give non-verbal signals. But to interpret these signals exactly, you need to stop the automated decision mechanism and evaluate the experiences. To understand its true significance, body language needs to be learned in context, interpreted in groups, analyzed for continuity with what is spoken, measured for continuity, and screened for cultural factors.

Filter the first experience

Non-verbal cues play a vital role in allowing us to make brief observations. Our ability to do this is one of our fundamental survival instincts. At the same time, our brains are hard-wired to react immediately to such non-verbal stimuli. This mechanism was set up a long time ago when our ancient ancestors faced risks and obstacles that were very different than those we face in today's modern society. Today, life is more complicated, with layers of social constraint and ambiguous interpretations added to the intricacy of our interpersonal relations. This is particularly true in the workplace, where organizational culture adds its complexities — a diverse collection of constraints and behavioral rules. Although first observations cannot always be right, you may enhance the ability to read someone's body language by going through the five C's: context, clusters, unity, continuity, and culture.

Context

Imagine this situation: a cool winter evening with light snowfall and a north blowing wind. You see a lady you know she's a co-worker sitting on a bench at a bus station. Her head is down, her eyes are closely closed, and she's slumped, trembling slightly and hugging herself. Now the scene changes: the same woman is in the same physical role. And instead of sitting outside on a bench, she's lying behind her desk in the office next to yours. Her body language is the same: head down, eyes closed, slumped over, shuddering, and hugging herself. The non-verbal signs are the same, but the current environment has changed your interpretation of those signs. She's gone

from informing you in a flash, "I'm so cold!
"To say," I am in pain. The sense of non-verbal communication varies as the context shifts. As in real estate, location counts. We can't try to grasp the actions of others without understanding the conditions in which the behavior happened. As our example shows, the message sent by that woman's body language shifted drastically based on whether she was seated outdoors in the cold or alone in her office. And certain conditions need more formal actions that may be viewed quite differently in some other environment.

When people communicate, a lot of the context is dictated by their interaction. The same man talking to a customer, a supervisor, or a manager will have a very different body language. Duration of day, assumptions based on previous experiences, and when contact takes place in a private or public setting — all these factors form the context in which body language happens. They need to be taken into account when determining significance. The key is to evaluate if non-verbal conduct is relevant to the context in which it happens. Dave and Diane, for example, have been friends and coworkers for years. As such, they stood next to each other, kept good eye contact, tapped each other on the shoulder, and always laughed during their discussions at the office. No one thought to comment on this before Diane revealed her relationship with another employee in the same organization. Equipped with that detail, the next time a colleague saw Dave and Diane laughing and enjoying each other's business. He said, "Careful now, and she's engaged. The background of the relationship had abruptly altered. Apparently, the non-verbal actions that Dave found acceptable when Diane was "alone" was now regarded as a potential issue.

Clusters

Non-verbal cues are a collection of gestures, postures, and behaviors that emphasize a common point in an expression cluster. A single gesture may have multiple meanings or indicate none at all (sometimes a cigar is just a cigar), but when you pair the single gesture with other non-verbal symbols, the meaning becomes clearer. An individual may cross his arms for a variety of reasons, but when a move is combined with a scowl, a headshake, and his legs turned away from you, you have a composite picture and a justification for inferring that he is resistant to anything you have just suggested. Always note to search for conduct clusters. The cumulative action of an individual is much more revealing than a particular gesture perceived separately. A smart person starts every meeting of workers by taking off his jacket, and he selects a chair in the middle of the conference table (not at the head). These actions alone would send a message of informality, but it is the rest of his movements that push the point home. Whenever anyone talks at the conference, the boss steps in with a look of curiosity on his forehead, smiles in agreement and gives the speaker full eye contact. Symbolically, this cluster of motions sets the tone for just what the discussion needs to be an open sharing of thoughts and questions.

Correspondence

Classic research reveals that the overall effect of a speech is based on 7% of the words used, 38% of the voice tone, and

55% of the facial expressions, hand movements, body posture, and other modes of non-verbal contact. You can't hear a human speak a foreign language and understand 93% of what is being conveyed. Even you can bet that when verbal and non-verbal channels of communication are out of balance, people — especially women — are likely to focus on non-verbal messaging and ignore verbal material. When feelings and actions are in tune, you see that they are substantiated in their body language. Their movements and actions are following what they mean. You may also see incongruity, where movements contradict words: a side-to-side headshake when saying yes or someone frowning and looking at the ground when telling you she's glad.

Consistency

You ought to know the basic actions of a person under comfortable or usually stress-free environments so that you can correlate them with the behaviors and movements that occur when the person is under stress. What's his usual way of looking about, sitting, standing while he's relaxed? How does he react when he addresses a non-threatening issue? Knowing someone's behavioral baseline strengthens the ability to detect major variations. One of the techniques employed by skilled police interrogators to diagnose dishonesty is to pose a set of non-threatening questions when watching how the person acts while there is no need to lie. Then, as more complicated group problems are approached, the officers look for shifts in non-verbal actions that suggest deceit at critical points. We all have trouble attempting to determine the consistency of someone we've just met.

Culture

This non-verbal interaction is informed by our cultural history, which is explored at length. Right now, it's important to realize that when reading body language, you should consider the levels of tension that the person is under. That's because the higher the emotional intensity, the more likely culture-specific expressions would pop up. Besides, body language is influenced by the various subcultures of which we are a participant—taking your pose, for example. Ballet dancers are taught to keep their bodies chest-forward, so you can always see them standing together with their heels and pointed toes (an adjusted first position). The most office staff are round-headed with a slight sag in their chests from hours spent hunched over their keyboards. Military forces also have a shoulder-back, spine-straight pose even after their service tour has finished. People from different parts of the same world can also use their bodies in a somewhat different way.

Take, for example, the rapidly changing pace of a modern New Yorker, and compare it with someone from the South's more relaxing gait. Note the possible variations in body language between a prototypically reserved and formal Young Englander and his more relaxed California counterparts. The more you know about a person's history, activities, and preferences, the more you can understand why those movements or postures are part of his particular repertoire — and why a break from these habits is important. Often people change their postures as they change topics.

Remember the five Cs — context, clusters, unity, continuity, and culture — as you're reading through the rest of this book. There is no question that people use non-verbal interactions to show their state of mind. Yet interpreting body language is not only about studying non-verbal signals; it is also about understanding how to get to the true meaning behind those signals.

CHAPTER 2: MANIPULATION: "TO REGULATE, MANIPULATE OR MANAGE"

"Manipulation" means that no matter what strategy you use to persuade others, you're manipulating them. Whenever you persuade someone to do what you're proposing other than what they want to do, you're influencing them. The term manipulation has many different interpretations, some of which can be perceived as disruptive. To impact someone or something is not evil in itself. It can only be harmful if it is meant to hurt someone or create problems. My use of the term deception is to be able to do the following thing:

- To regulate our behaviors, values, and attitudes through self-suggestion and self-hypnosis.
- To be able to manipulate with a degree of intensity to persuade others to come to our way of thought or doing something.
- To be able to place others in a position of benefit where the outcomes are a win/win for all the people concerned and are mutually agreeable.

The idea of using your sense of control to manipulate others is as ancient as our culture, without getting through all the details of Hypnosis, Trance Induction,

Energy Modulation, etc. Here you will find an elementary description of what hypnotherapy and trance is and how you can use it.

Manipulation is fascinating, and motivational behavior. It's not manipulation, it's not just intimidation, and it's not really like deceit. It is a common phenomenon in nearly all areas of life. Politics, architecture, culture, and even intimate relationships. However, technical literature, which aims to resolve the difficulty of systematically characterizing and evaluating the very essence of the phenomena, remains inadequate. Very few academic studies have been undertaken to examine, analyze, and clarify the underlying importance of manipulation and its significance compared to other driving behavior. Most of the literature that aims to confront this problem takes the concept together and summarizes it in one final description. We want to start the discussion of manipulation by introducing three ideas that have much helped me to understand the essential aspects of manipulation, particularly in exploring the uniqueness of the phenomenon and the secrets behind its strong effect. Most people would discern bribery from intimidation, on the one hand, and oppression. Researchers highlight the complexities of the phenomena and suggest the following difficult definition: "An effort to control when A attempts the dynamic motive of S's actions through manipulation or by relying on the supposed vulnerability of S.

Many of these philosophers focus on various critical features and elements of deception, including complexity (Rudi now), trickery (Godin), and irrational patterns (Phillips). These variations tend to bring into motion the impossibility of gathering and summarizing the very nature of deception in one definitive and straightforward description. There will still be actual examples of manipulations (or, more specifically, what we intuitively categorize as manipulative behavior) that contradict any concept. At least do not fall within the meaning of that description.

Manipulation produces an idea of free choice

The manipulation aims to manipulate the object to act in a direction that, under normal conditions, it is likely to prevent. Besides, specific deceptive tactics are designed to drive the target to respond in a way that is not compatible with its purpose, motives, and best interests. This trait of deceptive conduct is somewhat paradoxical. On the one hand, forcing someone to behave against their desires and interests suggests that manipulation involves persuasive elements. On the other hand, the word deception itself, synonymous with an enigmatic definition such as "maneuvering," indicates some judgment and thought as it works? This conflict can be overcome by incorporating the "illusory free choice" aspect to our definition of coercive interaction.

In general, the skilled manipulator tries to intrude, intervene, and control the decision-making process of the subject by giving him the idea that he (the issue) takes his behavior freely and independently. To accomplish this result, the manipulator tries to maneuver the target to see the "intentional intervention" (i.e., the manipulator) as the best alternative possible in the current scenario. Following our simple assumptions, particularly those of optimizing expectations and mitigating risk, the target is obliged to take the best possible action in the light of its understanding of the circumstance. The realistic sense is that the target, subject to unseen manipulation, assumes that its decisions are taken openly and independently. Hiding the necessary facts to produce the desired decision exemplifies the concept of "illustrious free choice" in a deceptive relationship. The goal, which assumes that it chooses the right choice honestly and objectively, is, in fact, subject to unseen intervention in its judgment and rational thought.

Unfortunately, it is not impossible to envision opposite circumstances where a person is persuaded that he or she is on the right track, making the correct choices and not considering alternative alternatives. Ironically, and even paradoxically, encouraging him to explore the value of other possibilities involves applying unorthodox methods of control that some deceptive techniques can deliver. In the most challenging situations, the person is stuck in a skewed perception of the truth that he is not able to analyze objectively. There are several classic examples: an enthusiastic young gentleman who is determined to become a great musician even though he lacks any sense of rhythm; a brave soldier who refuses to believe that the enemy is going to attack; a conscientious businessman who wastes much of his money, time and effort to increase the quality of products that are no longer in demand.

Cases of tragic entanglement are expensive in that they restrict the world's view of the trapped man, disrupt his adaptation to the ever-changing conditions of life, and bring much hardship and suffering to him and his surroundings. The critical point is that, under certain situations, an innovative, manipulative technique will often be the only hope. An indirect form of control will convince the ingrained target to challenge the legitimacy of its bias. In this way, the manipulator could enable the entrenched objective to consider other possibilities that it had not yet accepted. Ironically, in its initial role, the target was persuaded that it was selecting the best possible option, while deceptive pressure allowed it to make the right decision. I mark this kind of "manipulation emancipation' technique,' and I'm discussing it thoroughly in the coming chapters. Here, I would like to note briefly that this approach includes methods of control in psychotherapy and education that are intended to give the impression that the aim is to make the best of the transition by it.

He should not note that someone else (i.e., the psychiatrist or the educator) is actually maneuvering the circumstance and invisibly helping him find the path towards transformation and progress. In the following pages, we would need to discuss various issues relevant to this strategy: how could the benevolent manipulator accomplish this effect? Is "democracy by manipulation" still a successful system? What are the dangers involved?

Manipulation is hidden with the target

Motivating by using a persuasive technique is meant to mitigate the likelihood of goal objecting to the movements of the manipulator. The manipulator tries to discourage the target from contemplating such organizational options. Instead, the manipulator attempts to manipulate the target to justify potential actions that it (the target) refuses to acknowledge. The manipulator tries to create a motivational result smoothly and elegantly. He wishes to make the impression that the target is choosing his actions freely and independently (i.e., illusionary free choice). This effect could be achieved because, in the time of a manipulative interaction and the context of its subject, the manipulator's spectrum of vision is larger than the target's. It seems that the manipulator simply knows more. One of the functional consequences is that, at the moment of contact, the manipulator will change the point of view of the target, something that the target (who has a narrower range of vision) cannot do. The eventual inference is that, during a coercive relationship, the object cannot recognize that it works under a coercive control. A clear example of this is the act of seduction for indecent reasons.

The sophisticated seducer forecasts potential reactions to her future movements.

And she thinks like a target when she's planning a con. However, the target, whose mind is overwhelmed by intense emotions of desire and affection, does not even consider the risk of being led astray. The willingness of the target to recognize the true motives of the manipulator allows it to explore alternatives other than the objective of the manipulator. This is just what the manipulator tries to prevent; otherwise, it will do. Don't choose to exploit it. The realistic sense is that the "scam" has been revealed, and the target may determine whether or not it wants to yield or fail to behave in compliance with the instructions of the manipulator. In other words, it's not a matter of "illusory free choice" but a genuinely free choice.

As a consequence, the coercive act fails or does not occur. According to our interpretation, comments like "you exploit me" are self-contradictions. It is not possible to be a survivor of manipulation and to speak about it at the same time. In comparison, this aggressive strategy may have been used to shift positions in interaction.

Effects of manipulation on the essential power

The critical capability is an essential function that allows us to choose our behaviors according to our goals and desires. It's expected to act as a devoted guard whose job is to hold our actions and conduct following our self-interest and world-view. A motivating activity designed to lead a person to work contrary to their preferences without noticing the distortion must interrupt, or at least bypass, the inspection process. As a consequence, manipulative actions inevitably seek to influence the strong potential of the goal. I have described two types of techniques that are intended to accomplish this impact. The first one is planned to cloud, blur, and reduce the vital power of the target while the second, unexpectedly, is oriented towards increasing the efficiency of the target. The first type is pretty straightforward. During the confrontation, the manipulator uses morally objectionable methods to mitigate potential objections to his target movements. However, as the following two examples illustrate, specific and even competing motives and intentions can be used to influence elemental power. It could be used for the advantage of the manipulator and to boost the position of the target.

Persuasion & Hypnotic Effect is almost like learning a foreign language

When you continue to take the ideas of this book and incorporate them, you're going to have to put off "travel time," which means that you're going to have to clock in hours with a clear goal and get the benefits of your preparation. In reality, many of the ways you learn how to form your language and sentences can run counter to how you communicate at the moment. This will force you to have to stretch your imagination to comprehend the context of the ideas taught.

Mental Rehearsal: You should be an actor

When an actor appears on stage or in front of a screen, do you think they write their lines or use a script? The actor uses a script to practice their lines. When you continue to understand the boundaries of being able to convince or persuade, it's the same thing. You're going to have to practice the lines. Even when an actor puts on a person in the part they play, you're going to have to do the very same thing. You'll need to get out of your new comfort zone and start behaving outside the cage.

Get Out of the Comfort Zone

Everyone's in a safe spot. The purpose of this training is, above all else, the self-influence that you can gain to drag yourself out of your comfort zone. The comfort zone is the location, the mental state where you are residing in your mind. You need to have a mentality that you can sacrifice a bit to get the most value from this exercise. The rewards of this would well outstrip any discomfort you may face by studying it, but this internal training is the secret to concentrating on what you want, not what you don't want.

Start with the objective in mind

- What are you pretending to be?
- Where do you want to go?
- Who would you like to be involved with?
- What kind of job, company, or profession do you want?

This and several other questions are what you need to ask yourself because you know what you expect from this scenario of Hypnotic Manipulation and Hidden Intimidation. Set the target of where you want to be, the kind of skills you want to learn, and then post the date and focus. When the target is set, you should then reflect on how you're going to get there. Some have used this technique to become

Stage Hypnotists. At the same time, some have used these techniques to find anyone of the opposite sex. And many more have used these essential ideas to build a lifestyle that exists within their minds and enables them to benefit from all aspects of life, from work or company to any relationship they have.

Become a Controller

The significant thing I'm explaining here is to show you how you can become a master. The manager is the guy who's going to call the shots in his life. If you get nothing but this idea from this book, it will be worth reading. Being a planner is a mind focused on the facts, although you assume, they are not really as they are now. To be a controller is a state of consciousness.

The Controller's Behavior

The Alpha is the controller. He or she is the key man or woman, the "Target Maker." This is the mindset that you are going to build when you continue the process. Don't ever make the opposite idea happen in your mind. You are "A Controller." This is something you need to affirm to yourself regularly. "I'm in the process of being a strong controller" "I'm the controller in all aspects of my life."

Pre-play & Rehearse Performance

Always set it on your mind to make a replay of success. Your conscious mind is potent, and you can draw from it so much energy than you can ever imagine. It's this confidence that's going to drive you to your idea of what success means to you. The subconscious does what it's supposed not to do what it's intended to do. That's why you're going to have to use replay to adjust it.

Regulation of Anxiety

The critical question I have from people is that they are sometimes scared to try these techniques to see if they will work. After all, we're doing a lot of this secretly, so it makes sense that you're still reluctant to use a new strategy or method. Bear in mind what was said about becoming an actor before. You've got to get into your job and make yourself happy at times. Consider this as you control the discomfort of the unknown. "It's not the absence of fear, but the overcoming of fear." It's taking action. The more effort you take, the more fear you lose. Everyone's scared. It's all going to be focused on the target ahead.

All knowledge is state-dependent

Whenever you discover something, it depends on what kind of situation you're in at the moment. When you understand that touching a hot stove makes you burn, you've learned a valuable lesson. Every time after that, as you get close to a hot stove, your subconscious can immediately warn you of the condition and keep your hands away from the fire. We're learning from our:

-Physiology

-Emotional Conditions

So that means, to comprehend those things, if you can place yourself in a mental condition like any time you've learned something or the same emotional state, then it's a possibility why you can understand it much better.

Body Language That Can Make You More Convincing and Pleasant

Will you want to reassure someone to be seen as more likable? You do, of course! Here's an easy and effective way to make this possible. Do you want to learn about a body language method that can boost your likability and effect over others? There is such a mechanism, known as "Mirroring." This interpersonal communication strategy would help you to communicate with, connect with, and build confidence and respect in the mind of the person you're talking to. This isn't bad for the body language element that isn't on other people's radar screens. Body language is not just essential to get the message across. It also plays a part in how people view you and how you feel for yourself! From career interviews and in-person and interactive meetings, you learn more than you can.

The Strength of Body Language to Facilitate Person-to-Person Interactions

Mirroring involves copying the stance, the gestures, the verbal skills, and the vocabulary of the person you speak in interpersonal conversation. How is it working? A 2016 study using functional MRI showed that speakers and listeners "reacted and adapted to each other's signals." This result was published in The Wall Street Journal on the advantages of mirroring, especially in industry. This resonated deeply with me because it was the foundation of traditional acting practice. The exercise is called Mirror and shows the same impact on the person-to-person interactions that the theoretical experiment has confirmed, even without costly equipment. In Mirror, one person (Person "A") stands in front of an imaginary mirror and moves instinctively

("Getting ready for the day" or "Arguing an argument" are appropriate examples here). Usually, this person is advised to step slowly. "A" is companion (Person "B") faces "A" and copies everything he does. The practice can be stepped up by telling "A" that he is unconsciously talking to himself. Again, "B" would imitate all that "A" is doing (and, in the second edition, the facial expression). The functions are often changed, often several times.

The fascinating thing about the Mirror exercise is that intention, sentiment, expressiveness, and energy level are all exposed by expression and movements. This is an invaluable lesson in itself for practicing artists. Equally significant, it is a fast-track illustration of the interconnectedness of human beings and how it can be fostered by exhibited and imitated actions. Both experiences are as invaluable to public speakers as to stage actors.

How to Develop Interpersonal Speech Report and Trust?

How do you use mirroring productively in your discussions and relationships with others? The secret to this is the sincerity with which you pursue and execute the technique. You should begin by not trying to mimic your conversational partner at all. Instead, work on knowing what the other person is thinking about and what their desires tend to be. If you stay open and fully involved in what the other has to suggest, you will improve your ability to practice mirroring. That is, if you are trustworthy of your purpose, what you present to your partner will come out of honesty rather than an attempt to exploit. As for the technique itself, begin by matching the voice tone and rhythm of the other person. Vocal signals are typically more precise than body movements and can serve to ease the first attempt at mirroring. Enable yourself to imitate non-verbal habits that you see. It may include posture and location, whether the person is sitting forward or lying back in the chair, the level of eye contact, head nodding or pacing, and the level of involvement or enthusiasm expressed emotionally and at the rate of the individual's voice.

Act to get the best outcomes spontaneously and genuinely

The theory is that you just want to be involved in what the other person does. Your speech, body, and emotional engagement represent that degree of dedication. You can be shocked how energized and concentrated you become in a conversational context. If that happens, you might forget that you practice mirroring at all. Mirroring can yield off in terms of knowing and listening to the person you're referring to. But it's also valuable teaching to simply become a more reflective person, one who reflects on others rather than on himself.

Persuade how to use body language in a convincing argument?

Whenever you're communicating, the material lies on the surface for everyone to see. But beneath that visible surface flows a healthy river of influence. The undercurrent that viewers can't as clearly identify: the influential underneath generated by non-verbal contact—these aspects of interpretation and power of the preceding language. In some instances, we can't name them or describe their exact influence at all.

Yet they still work throughout and under the familiar pieces of our speeches and presentations. Among the most important of these is body language. A good speaker must learn how to make the most of the body's language, for the body is an important communication medium. As speakers, we are bodies traveling through space, and audiences respond as strongly to what they see and understand from body language as they do to any other aspect in our speech. Here are four ways to use body language and talk with greater force and convince, empower, and encourage audiences. Three of these tips are about the sort of expression you're talking about in terms of your appearance. The fourth is a vital body language technique that you would use in any conversation, voice, or presentation you give in public.

For speaking when you stand

- **Ground yourself.** Stand with the legs apart at the armpit-width to establish a comfortable and calm appearance. In results, you get a portion of your energy out of the world. Don't be stripped of the power.

- **Move with Intent.** Too many speakers are walking, pacing, or going without Intent. Choose parts of the stage for some of the critical topics you address, and use visual aids and even crowds to give the message a tangible representation.

- **Make massive Signs Restricted.** The single expression that amplifies an essential argument is the one that gives value to it. Make it clean, and it's limited. Too regular or slow movements do not offer any physical expression to the above.

- **Do use facial gestures.** In part, the listeners determine whether to trust someone with facial gestures or look in the eyes of the speaker. An expressionless speaker has offered the crowd too little to move on.

For speaking while you're sitting down

- **Shift the back of the chair.** Getting too relaxed in a chair is a risk while you're talking. When you need to express motivation and enthusiasm, you need to go on, which is humiliating.

- **Get up and take Lean Forward.** Strong stance when sitting displays composure and brings authority. Leaning forward is an essential hint to your audience that you are committed and involved.

- **Open yourself for yourself.** A common mistake among speakers sitting at a board table is to hold their hands together or keep their arms in a "closed" pose. This establishes a physical distance between you and your audience.

- **Gesture.** Just because you're sitting down does not mean you can't make a move. Too many speakers become talking heads and do not have amplifying or encouraging motions. Always use your arms and your hands.

When you speak practically

- **Stand and move on.** Audiences who you talk to physically or over the phone can hear the emotional expressiveness that you use when you speak. If you intend to engage yourself when you talk in person entirely, why do you remove movement while you chat on the phone or in a webinar?

- **Use headphones**. Not only can the headphones set you up to switch and talk, but they make your voice sound louder and more substantial. When you fall in the rhythm, you're not going to want to be around them.

- **Try to ask questions.** Although listeners can't respond to the visual cues you send them (such as when they should respond), you need to send these cues outspokenly. You and your audience are going to feel like you're connected. And you're trying to get the audience out of multitasking!

- **Use speech power.** In the lack of essential contextual cues, the vocal capacity has to be consumed. And no movements for the audience to see.

They need the voice to point and focus. Here are the 5 Main Techniques for Vocal Modulation to help you render more effective expression and presentations.

Observe the body language of the crowd

- **Focus the Energies Outward, not inward.** The body language coming from your audience is as essential as the non-verbal feedback you're sending. Don't care about how you're doing — watch how your listeners respond.

- **Take a look at how listeners react.** When you observe such motions, expressions, eye contact, and jiggling legs, pay attention as the patterns change. It's also a warning that you're losing the attention of listeners.

- **Change your rhythm and approach as appropriate**. When that happens, change what you do. Say a story if you've been talking in general; give an example; or turn off the system you're using or start using if you've been talking for too long.

- **Develop Interaction.** Keep the audience engaged above all. It may mean merely using body language, putting them on their feet, or engaging in an exercise. Audiences are often more convinced, empowered, and encouraged as they perform, not only listen.

CHAPTER 3: USE OF BODY LANGUAGE FOR PERSUADING

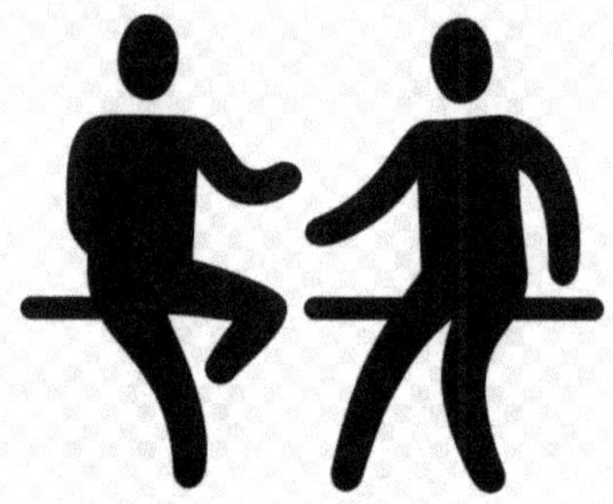

Ever listen to someone talking and remember that something doesn't ring true about that person? Everything was in disagreement with his words and the way he handled himself. That may have been his reluctance to look you in the eye. Perhaps his hands have overwhelmed you. Or maybe it was facial movements that didn't reflect what he was saying? No, now you know it was his position; focused, honest people just don't conduct themselves that way. As you will see, the body tells a tale of its own. You will also do that.

- Listen and read others.
- Make sure whether the person is trustworthy or someone you're right to run away from right now.

The eyes do not deceptive

Have you ever spoken to someone who isn't looking straight at you? The person stared over your back, over your head, on the street, or at someone else anywhere except you. What did you make about that? The person made you upset with that. Very possibly, you doubted the person's purpose, integrity, and trust. Or you might have been neglected. Eye communication plays a vital role in how people view each other, and, as a speaker, you should pay particular attention to it. If you make eye contact with your audience, they will believe you're genuine, trustworthy, polite, and truthful. These emotions have a significant influence on how listeners interpret the message.

There are other advantages of eye contact:

- It helps you to create a relationship with listeners.
- It's catching their interest.
- It reveals that you speak frankly.
- Demonstrates self-confidence.
- Indicates that you're responsive.
- Recognizes individuals.

While communicating with a group of people:

- Look at the crowd before you start the speech.
- Check from one hand to the other before you speak.
- Communicate and respond to one user at a time.
- Keep your eye contact for 3 to 4 seconds for each individual.
- Use four connections, connect, chat, and begin.

Stop eye contact includes:

- Staring at one person for so long.
- Looking over the heads of the participants.
- Staring up at the roof or out of the window.

Show Commitment and Passion by Hand Gestures

Hand gestures are the most articulate component of the body's language. Make your hand movements above your elbow and away from your body to be most successful. They should be robust and healthy to demonstrate confidence and excitement. A sweeping wave of your arm to show space would bring more to the message than a half-hearted gesture of the hand. Hand movements can also be absolute and varied rather than minimal and repetitive; having the same action over and over is annoying. Make the hand motions smaller for large crowds so that even people at the back of the room can see them.

Display some simple hand gestures:

- Height, weight, form, direction, and location.
- Value or urgency.
- Comparing and Contrasting.

Hand movements to stop include the following:

- The parent pointing number.
- Fist, rage and stress.
- The karate chop is brutal.

Example hand placements shall include:

- Split palms, one is holding the other at the waist.
- Hand to foot, able to make a move.

Always sure that your facial expression matches your speech

Your face unconsciously conveys hints as to how the listeners are expected to respond or behave. When you're talking about a horrific traffic wreck, but you're laughing and nodding, the viewers would be curious, not upset. Your facial expression must be compatible with the emotions or details of your interaction.

Assume the rooted role of the Express Trust

- The position you hold while still standing is significant because it shows your level of trust and comfort. If you slouch your shoulders and fix your eyes on the pavement, the audience will think you're timid and frail. If you continuously change your weight from one foot to another, you look awkward and anxious, and your movement can distract your audience. But when you stand upright, your legs shoulder-length apart, with your weight equally balanced over each leg, with gaze squarely at your audience, you express trust and poise.

- It's called the rooted position. Imagine that the feet are firmly embedded in the earth. It's not going to be easy for you to sway or get off balance. This is the state of strength and wealth.

How to persuade people by using psychological theories?

Influence the crowd with these ideas without becoming sleazy about it. Here is a summary of each of the ten hypotheses, which may sound familiar to you. Because you've used them in the past or because you've had someone attempt them on you.

1) Hypothesis of Enhancement

When you show a particular behavior, your mentality hardens. The reverse is also true, communicating ambiguity softens the action.

2) Theory of conversion

The minority in a group will have a detrimental impact on the influence of those in the majority. Usually, those among the majority who are more vulnerable are those who could have entered because it was convenient to do so, or who thought like there were no alternatives. Consistent and positive minority voices are the most powerful.

3) Theory of Intelligence Processing

This idea entails a convincing person purposely violating one of the four conversational maxims. What are the four of them?

• Quantity: The details are complete and accurate.

• Quality: The material is real and reliable.

• Relationship: The information is essential to the discussion.

• Style: Detail is conveyed in an easy-to-understand style, and non-verbal acts reflect the sound of the sentence.

4) Priming up

You can be affected by factors that influence your understanding of short-term thoughts and behavior. Here's a very creative example of Transforming Minds. A stage magician says 'ask' and 'repeat' in separate sentences in the priming of a human to dream about the term 'tricycle' later.

5) Reciprocity norm

Widespread social practice, and reciprocity, requires our duty to share the advantages to others.

6) Principle of availability

I want to see what's in the short stock. This motivation grows when you foresee the disappointment you may have if you skip it by not moving quickly enough.

7) Sleeper Consequences

Persuasive communications appear to reduce persuasiveness over time, except for low-credibility communications. Messages that begin with low persuasion gain conviction as our minds steadily disassociate the source from the content (i.e., potentially a sleazy car dealer and his guidance on what the best car is).

8) External effects

We are heavily motivated by others based on how we interpret our interaction with the influencer. Social evidence on a web file, for example, is convincing if the testimonials and advice come from reputable outlets, major companies, or peers.

9) Change in Yale Mentality Approach

This approach, based on many years of study by Yale University, has identified a variety of convincing speech variables, including being a confident, competent speaker, whether it is essential to first or last, and ideal communities to approach.

10) Absolute terms and conditions

Some words hold more significant influence than many others. This definition splits the applicable term into three categories:

God's names: those words that bring blessings or require obedience/sacrifice. For example, development, importance.

Devil's words: certain words that are hated and provoke contempt, such as racist and pedophile.

Charismatic words consist of those terms that are vague, less measurable than either the names of Heaven or the Demon.

7 Forms Compelling Body Gestures Reinforce Company Presentations

If you're presenting a new plan to clients or heading a regular sales meeting within your own company, presentations are moments of your professional career. The basis of a fantastic presentation is your content, and the more you plan, the greater the end outcome will be. Still, there is another aspect of the overall performance as a presenter and implementing your presentation. Talk honestly with poise and elegance, and a decent performance will be a win. On the other hand, poor execution will undermine the efficacy of otherwise excellent materials. To make the most of your content and put yourself on top of it, consider these seven creative body language hacks.

Arrange your pose like a Superman

Before your speech starts, take some time in your bathroom or another private place to practice the best Superman pose. Step up straight on your chest. Either put your hands on your shoulders with your elbows extended or lift your arms above your head in a triumphant pose. The trick is to make you look and sound as big as you can. Doing this for a few minutes before a big event would inevitably make you feel more comfortable, which, in turn, would motivate your presentation?

Stand up straight

Squatting can be a difficult habit to break, but it's essential to do so if you want to look at your best during the presentation. Give the statement standing erect on the back of the head. Be careful not to widen your shoulders or exaggerate your height, but to straighten your frame. This has two clear advantages. Next, you will become more assured to your audience, which will increase the appeal of your content. Second, the airway will be balanced, and you can automatically sound louder and smoother.

Open up your muscles

It is necessary to keep your posture open. You can feel both more optimistic and more trustworthy to your audience, even though it is just on a subconscious basis. Don't stretch your arms over your body or place your hands in your back. Do not cross your legs and lean against the wall, either. Keep the arms free and comprehensive to show that you are a free individual. Your message is going to be best received.

Take a look in the eyes of the audience

Eye contact is a vital aspect of body language and behavioral guidance for one-on-one sessions, such as work interviews and business talks. Still, it is also helpful in a comprehensive presentation setting. When you communicate with a big group of people, you can't look at everyone's eyes at once. Instead, reflect on the principal members of the group and look in their eyes. Don't keep it for longer than a few seconds; switch around the room to reach as many participants as possible. Doing so adds an extra special touch to your pitch and reveals that you're genuinely involved in your audience.

Move around comfortably

The stage is your domain, so make use of it. Don't make this mistake of staying in one position, even though it's on the podium. Instead, walk around the stage to take as much room as possible. You would look more relaxed, more assured, more familiar in your surroundings. It also helps the speaker to be reflected in various ways.

Use your hands

Get the hands involved in the talk to improve your arguments and keep the viewer's more involved. Place your finger in your palm so that you can bring a reference around. Open your hands to show ambiguity or indicate involvement. Possible gestures and implementations are unrestricted, so use them sparingly. Using hand motions very much can make you seem anxious or agitated. Using the same movements over and over again might make you seem gimmicky or repetitive. Instead, use various forms of expressions, and only at times of presentation that you need an additional "oomph."

Relax the facial muscles

People are searching for visual clues to the feelings, motives, and trustworthiness of another person. It doesn't affect performing in front of a vast crowd. To optimize the meaning and efficacy of what you say, keep your facial expressions loose as you pass through various areas of the presentation. It can make you sound more genuine and individual, which goes a long way towards persuading the viewer. Of course, it's not enough to understand these body language patterns. If you want to be genuinely successful in their implementation without acting like an insane guy, you will have to do it in the real world. Adjust it until it looks and seems familiar to you. They'll be a regular part of your speaking patterns before you know it, and you'll never have to think about them again.

CHAPTER 4: STRATEGIC INTERPRETATION OF BODY LANGUAGE

What you're doing reflects just about half of what people hear. According to research, 55% of the message you convey comes from your body language. That's why understanding body language has such a long tradition. Over the last century, psychology has made a great deal of progress in understanding the various social implications of body language. Below are some of the most important observations.

The shake of the shoulder is a familiar gesture not to know what's going on

According to a study, everybody is shrugging the shoulder. The shrug is a "simple example of a common expression used to indicate that a person doesn't know or understand what you're doing." It's a different move that has three essential parts, and they're all going on. The palms open to reveal what is enclosed in the hands, the shoulders hunched to shield the throat from attack, and the brow lifted, a traditional, and submissive greeting.

Open palms are a typical example of authenticity

Ever note how, when anyone swears to tell the truth in a court of law, they place one hand on a sacred document and hold their other hand in the air, palm in front of everyone they're referring to? An open palm has been connected to "truth, integrity, patriotism and obedience" in Western history. "Just like a dog shows its throat to demonstrate obedience or yield to a victor," people use their hands to indicate that they are vulnerable and not a threat.

A pointing finger with a closed hand is an attempt to assert superiority

When someone closes their hand and points with their index finger, they attempt to show superiority, but it doesn't always succeed. The Palm-Closed-Finger-Pointing is a fist where the pointing finger is used as a suggestive weapon in which the speaker metaphorically beats his listeners into submission. Subconsciously, it evokes destructive emotions in others because it precedes a right overarm strike, a violent motion used by most primates in a physical attack.

Check for lack of wrinkles around the eyes to spot a false expression

A sincere smile, also known as a Duchene smile, is almost impossible to do on orders. That's why family pictures appear to look so uncomfortable. The grin, it turns out, is all about the crow's feet around your eyes. They crinkle as you smile joyfully. They're not because you're faking it. When someone pretends to look perfect, but they're not, you're not going to see the wrinkles.

Raised eyebrows are also indicators of distress

Much like real smiles form the lines around your eyes, research suggests worry, disappointment, or anxiety will cause people to lift their eyebrows in discomfort. So, if anyone acknowledges your new hairstyle or dress with their raised eyebrows, it might not be sincere.

They're probably concerned if their voice goes up or down

Either you know it or not, your vocal range indicates your curiosity. As soon as a discussion starts, besotted women turn into singing voices, Psychology Today states, "when men lower their octave."

If they mimic the language of your body, the conversation is generally going well

When two people get together, their postures and gestures mimic each other. When the closest friend of yours crosses their ankles, you will do the same. When you're on a date that's going great, you're both going to make the same ridiculous hand motions. This is how we mimic each other as we sense a bond.

Eye contact indicates curiosity, both positive and negative

When you look at someone in the eyes, it determines the body's state of enthusiasm. However, the perception of this stimulation depends on the individuals concerned and the circumstances.

But if they've been staring into your eyes for so long, they may be cheating

To stop becoming shifty-eyed, some liars would deliberately keep their eyes too long to make it mildly awkward. They can even stand still and not twitch.

Extensive posture signals strength and a feeling of accomplishment

How people hang on to themselves is a significant hint as to how they feel. Research has shown that broad poses improve testosterone and optimism. If they lay back and relax, they feel strong and in charge. Similarly, evidence reveals that even blind-born people raise their V-shaped arms and lift their head somewhat as they win a physical competition. On the other hand, a low-power posture seen as someone covers and wraps their arms around them raises cortisol, a stress hormone.

Crossed legs are typically a symbol of reluctance and low receptivity, which are a negative sign of bargaining.

There wasn't a single deal when one of the negotiators crossed his legs. Psychologically, crossed legs signify a person's mental, emotional, and physical closure — which could mean that they are less inclined to budge in negotiations.

A 'cluster' of movements reveals a strong sense of interaction

The attraction is not transmitted by a single signal, but by a chain.

Whether they laugh at you, they're definitely into you

If anyone is responsive to your jokes, they're typically interested in you. Evolutionary psychologists claim that laughter plays a central role in human growth. It acts as a means of signaling a desire for friendship, whether platonic or romantic.

A clenched jaw, a clenched neck, or a furrowed forehead indicates tension

Many of these are "limbic reactions" associated with the limbic system of the brain. Emotion, detecting and adapting to threats, and maintaining our safety are all the substantial duties of the limbic system. The bus leaves without us, and we're clenching our teeth, scratching our heads. We're called to work another day, and the circles of our eyes widen as our chin falls. Humans have been expressing pain this way for millions of years.

Expansive, influential positions demonstrate leadership

If they are natural or trained, there are various signs and actions people use when they believe they are a boss, or at least attempt to persuade you that they are. These include maintaining straight posture, walking confidently, steeping and palm-down hand movements, and typically accessible and flexible body postures.

A trembling leg signifies an unstable inner state

Your legs are the most significant part of your body, so when you walk, it's pretty hard for anyone not to notice. A trembling portion is a symptom of fear, frustration, or both.

Crossed weapons can indicate defensiveness, depending on the context

It's quick to grab body-language signals, but it's essential to be conscious of the context. Although crossed arms generally mean that someone is near, people are much more likely to cross their arms when it's cold, and their chair doesn't have an armrest. Be mindful of the surroundings before deciding or modifying a plan based on these types of behaviors.

Persuasive body language positions

Your body language cannot determine the effectiveness of your performance. A compelling body language makes the argument more convincing and engaging. At least, it's holding the interest of the public. Below is a situational persuasive body language proposed by the Center for Body Language.

The box position (trustworthy)

Early in Bill Clinton's political career, he would punctuate his remarks with bold, large expressions that made him seem untrustworthy. To help him keep his body language under control, his counselor taught him to visualize a box in front of his chest and abdomen, and to keep his hand going inside it. Since then, "Clinton Box" has become a common phrase in the industry.

To hold a ball (Dominant, commanding)

Showing as if you were holding a basketball in your hands is an indication of competence and power. As if you almost entirely have the truth at your hands. Some people use this role often in their speeches.

Pyramid-hands (relaxes, self-confidence)

When people are anxious, their hands flit about and fidget. They're still there when they're confident. One way to do so is to put your hands together in a comfortable pyramid. Often business executives use this gesture but beware of overuse or combining it with superior or dismissive facial expressions. The intention is to demonstrate that you're comfortable, not arrogant.

Wide stance (in control, confident)

How people stand is a good predictor of their mentality. When you stand in this calm and confident posture, with your legs about the width of your shoulder apart, it shows that you feel more in control.

Palms up (accepting, honest)

This gesture shows transparency and honesty. A lot of people make excellent use of this in their interviews. They are robust and prominent figures, but they still seem able to have a genuine relationship with the people they are talking to, be it a single person or a crowd of thousands.

Palms down (emphatic, strong)

The opposite trend can also be interpreted positively — as a symbol of dominance, power, and aggressiveness.

Proven Convincing Strategies

Presentations are a danger. You're spending precious time and effort, so you can't predict the nature of the production you'll be struggling with. The precise disposition of the crowd cannot be determined, or all the factors of the situation cannot be managed. You have to be brave to excel and come armed with an ace up your sleeve. You've got to be a master of convincing. And if your goal is merely to inspire or educate, you will need to convince your audience to pay attention. If you need to push your audience to take action, convincing is necessary.

Use your hands during a speech
Let your hands make a natural gesture during your speech. Research has shown that the commentators are judged to be more effective and knowledgeable when they make hand gestures compared to when they keep their hands still. When you're gesturing, be particularly mindful of how you use your hands. There are more interactions between the brain and the palm of the hands than any other part of your body. Palms have developed as an integral

component of human minds. The research reveals how a speaker's palm direction can send a signal that appeals to your primitive brain. Based on the signal being broadcast, the speaker will either win the support and interest of the audience or be dismissed by the audience. Palm orientation was evaluated in one of the case studies mentioned; the analysis concluded that the palm-up speaker had up to 40% more retention than the palm-down speaker. Speaking with your hands is going to make you more likable and convincing. If you address your palms down, you are going to be viewed as intimidating and commanding. The motion of the palms down appears threatening. The crowd laughs because the updated greeting is humorous.

Be a Wordsmith

Be careful with the words you chose to use during your presentations. For example, focus mainly on terms that can hit an emotional chord with members of the audience. Compared to terms with neutral connotations, inspirational words have a more profound impact on members of the audience. More specifically, the analysis was concluded. In the present investigation, we investigated whether there was a qualitative advantage of emotional memory relative to neutral words. The findings of six tests indicated that there was such a benefit: overall tasks, the specifics of the interpretation of terms (assessed by subjective and quantitative measures), were more likely to be recalled for emotional than neutral objects. Take the word healing to the next stage by adding some of the most popular terms into the presentations.

YOU

Use the verb "you" during the presentations want your audience excited. Rewrite sentences, substitute the "I" word with your word, to concentrate on the listener and not on yourself. Besides, if you give a presentation to quite a few individuals, start using their first names during the presentation. Don't push it through; be normal when approaching the members of the audience directly.

FREE

The word 'free' is continuously thrown into our faces by advertisers and service providers. And the term holds specific forces of persuasion. However, be cautious with your free usage to preserve the importance of your message, while still tapping into the significant energy of the word.

SUDDENLY

Suddenly, the term makes activities or interactions look thrilling and straightforward. If you can use the word frankly and tactfully as part of your call-to-action at the end of your presentation, go for it. The chances are that the performance will improve.

Tap the sensory experiences

Use the strength of the five senses to manipulate the system for the next presentation. For instance, if technological problems interrupt the performance, keep the crowd entertained by playing some fun music. Pleasant music played while you're on hold wants to keep guests on the line length to escape the challenge of trying to convince an irritated crowd, use music to keep people happy for you. Use colors strategically, and optimize the compelling value of the presentation design.

Storytelling presentation

Studies prove that tales are more convincing than rational claims. The most popular presentations are around 65 percent stories and 25 percent statistics, with the rest an illustration of the reputation.

Use the Sensitivity to Failure

Ask the crowd to think that you're doing the role that you want them to accomplish. As weird as it may seem, the brain simply cannot tell the difference between dreaming reality and witnessing reality. When the viewer imagines an experience, they have it both physically and psychologically. As a consequence, the group is less likely to condemn the response you are calling for. This is because our emotional reaction to loss is twice as strong as our pleasure of reward.

Be polite

Likable presenters are more convincing than presenters who are unable to relate to the audience. People tend to prefer speakers who are identical, generous with compliments, and cooperative. Before giving a presentation, study the audience deeply. When you take the stage, be prepared to express commonality between yourself and members of the crowd, and praise the group. When you work in the room following the lecture, comply with demands from members of the public who require a final drive for convincing. Comfort is another trait of welcoming leaders. Researchers report that leaders need to be viewed as warm, possibly more than professional, convincing. While projecting credibility is necessary, neglecting to show trustworthiness/warmth, a psychological force makes it quite difficult for leaders to acquire allegiance and be convincing sustainably. Among other methods, experts recommend flashing a genuine smile at critical times of your performance to create a warm atmosphere.

Gestures certainly matter how messages are processed and received. New research on the interactive tasks of movements offers some handy hints for persuading to live. And considering that the study is about talking to the hands, it's unsurprisingly enough, a group of Italian researchers introduced what is likely to be the first fully-controlled experiment to look into the convincing efficacy of hand movements in isolation. That alone was enough to get me to hand over the $34 to see what they find.

- First, you should make an expression. Irrespective of the form of gesture, gesturing is more convincing than not making gestures.

- Second, you should stop making gestures towards yourself. Pointing to one, keeping your hands on oneself, or even self-referencing, produced lower perceptions of the skill of the speaker.

- Third, the best gestures are "related to expression." In other words, instead of meaningless motions that do not have the requisite significance, the best gestures are those that are "ideal" to express or validate the concept. When speakers related their movements to expression, the participants in the study saw them as more successful and more composed.

Not only do the movements help the listener, but they also help the speakers. Another research showed that using gestures when illustrating the idea contributed to a greater comprehension and learning of the speaker. Currently, nothing in this or any other study that I am aware of indicates that it is a good idea to plan or practice for movements properly. If you are a well-trained performer, such actions are hurried and awkward, which is the opposite of the natural confidence that you want to express.

"Beats" (or "Rhythmic Gesture")

They are punctuated up and down or side to side movements that complement speech like a conductor's baton. Since they are not equivalent to voice, they are not the most powerful emotions. Often, to the degree that they can accompany some form of material, they can be a favorite speaker and a diversion for audiences. They may play an essential role: think of them as a simple way to run a highlighter over sections of your post. If you use them sparingly, and if you want to bust out one or two "beats" just before you hit a crucial stage, the audience will pay more attention and be more likely to recall the material.

"Points" (or "textual expressions")

The speaker doing these will suggest (with a finger, a fist, an arm, or even ahead) something present in the room. Since they are indeed connected to speaking, they are more powerful, more capable gestures. They're explicitly letting the listener see what you're talking about. The target is important: an occasional finger poke to the rival can be successful as long as it is pleasant and offensive, but pointing directly at the crowd can be perceived as impolite or superior. The most vital "points" may be towards an idea or a position, helping to bring into motion something that may otherwise be hypothetical.

"The Designs" (or the Iconic Gestures)

Here, speakers use their hands like a sculptor to signify some shape ("All names were put in a large, circular bowl") or some method ("Then he quickly climbed up the tree"). You can easily picture a speaker creating a bowl in the first case, or wiggling a few fingers to signify a climbing motion in the second. These are the most influential movements in the Italian analysis above since they are most specifically linked to the meaning of the voice. It's not that the viewer wants a gesture to grasp the idea (the bowls and the tree-climbing are common enough). The motion makes the audience imagine and therefore engage in the message rather than only receive it.

"Metaphors" (or Analog Gestures)

An expression acts as a metaphor as it relies on a philosophical association with the meaning of your voice. Rather than drawing a particular entity or mechanism (like the "type" above), it has a symbolic relationship to what you mean. For instance, a gesture suggesting support (e.g., the picture on the left) may be accompanied by a general message conveying some help. But the trick to this approach is subtlety: instead of "and that's why you should endorse [gesture] my friend," you'd want to retain a gesture like this when presenting a longer subject that is geared towards assistance. But you should make a motion in favor of the term, not an actual phrase.

"Placeholders" (or Unified Gesture)

These gestures promote the contact process by allowing the audience to hang messages together. In the way that a storyteller can follow the same facial action when speaking to a particular individual, movements can be used to delineate your text. For example, if you debate with opposing counsel during a bench meeting, your opponent cuts you off mid-sentence. You may hold your hands in the same up-and-coming role you were in before you were interrupted, as opposing counsel continues to signal that you did not give up the floor. Or, if you're faced with a judge's question that causes you to step away from the mainline of your case, you may drop the gesture you've been using, and then revive the same motion once you're through with the side-issue and back on the main track of your case.

Look at movements with this amount of clarity, it's convenient to say, "No thanks, I'm going to concentrate on content ..." but it's crucial to note that the audience is observing and listening. Material is the ruler, as should be the case in the legal phase, and natural distribution will always be the highest. But to think about the pieces of communication held by the hands and body, particularly as it relates to gestures, is an essential part of the whole image.

CHAPTER 5: SIGNIFICANCE OF BODY LANGUAGE IN PUBLIC DISCOURSE

No one should underestimate the importance of body language in public speaking and presentations. Pass out the wrong sensations, and you're going to end up driving the viewer away. Yet with the right body language, you will win them over just as quickly. Some people just try to get their speeches 'over and done with' without caring about movements and body language. It's essential for you to be cautious and want to hear more about how you can use body language to your benefit. When it comes to presentations, body language can make one successful or fail. We will excel if we learn and make fair use of our body language, and lose if we let our body language get the best. When you practice your voice, it's essential to focus on your body language as well. On the day of your presentation, you're going to be happy, relaxed, and assured that you've got what it takes to make your presentation excellent. Now, the thing is, there are two sides when it comes to body language presentations. There's the body language of the host (that's you), and there's the body language of the audience. Knowing how to read your audience is a unique ability that can come in handy later. You don't want to be one of those presenters who think they're doing an excellent job on stage when, in fact, their audience is boring to death.

The Empathy Theory

Part of the effect your physical activity has on the viewer can be demonstrated by the idea of empathy, the desire to express the thoughts or feelings of another person. When you talk, people in your audience appear to be representative of your attitudes. They instinctively sense what you're feeling and react accordingly. It is essential, therefore, that the body diligently reflects real emotions. If you look calm and secure, the audience will probably feel comfortable and optimistic. If you smile at your audience, they'll see you as a nice guy, and they'll smile back at you. Most notably, once they are persuaded that you are genuine and trustworthy, they will pay attention to what you say and judge it on their terms. Of course, this method will work the other way around. If you are uncomfortable, the viewers would probably be uncomfortable. If you frown – even unintentionally – your listeners will generally frown at you. If you don't smile at them, they're going to feel rejected. And if you avoid eye contact, they will sense a loss of self-control and lose trust in you and what you speak.

Why Physical Action Support?

When you show purposeful, constructive physical activity when speaking to the crowd, you have a real barometer of your emotions and attitudes. But there are also other benefits:

01.   Messages are more unforgettable than that

People become bored with static presentations. That's why TV newscasts nearly often have a clip depicting some type of action. If there is a crash, protest rally, or any other visually entertaining incident, the newscast would usually lead – even though it's not the most important news item. A newscast that focused on "talking heads" will quickly lose listeners who could get as much information from the TV. On the other side, it's impossible not to stare at a moving target. You've already heard how people pay attention to visual disturbances at Toastmasters gatherings. Late-comer arrivals or flickering timing lights typically siphon energy away from expression. People understand signals that hit several senses, too. We recall more of what we can see than what we can hear. However, we remember better when both our visual and our auditory senses are concerned. As a speaker, you can capitalize on these patterns by presenting visual stimulation that catches the interest of your audience and increases the reception of your verbal messages. Gestures, body gestures, facial expressions – both of these can be useful resources when done with skill.

02.   Punctuation gives value to it

Written language has a wide variety of message punctuation symbols: commas, intervals, exclamation marks, etc. But when you speak, you use an entirely new set of metaphors to remind the listener what the most critical aspects of your voice are and bring strength and energy to your expression. Any of them are presented with a speech. Gestures, body gestures, and facial expressions are just as efficient. However, to have the best potential effect, you need to organize your voice and body and function together. The more communication tools you use, the more efficiently you communicate.

03.   Nervous Stress transformed

To a certain degree, you are getting anxious before a speech is safe. It indicates that you care about doing well. All of the world's best entertainers readily agree that they're worried about success. Yet real fear — the kind that ruins a speech — will prevent you from being a successful speaker—anxiety and nervousness in public speaking practice at three levels: mental, emotional, and physical. The mental and emotional concerns are overcome by self-confidence – a by-product of training and practice. The easiest way to regulate the physical signs of anxiety and nervousness is by the deliberate use of gestures and body motions. The adrenal glands are stimulated in public speech. Your pulse is quickening. Your breathing gets shallower and quicker. Your muscles are stressed. Since the body can do anything to alleviate anxiety, you will unintentionally practice mannerisms that will distract the audience – so you can dissipate the tension. Gestures and body motions will help you take advantage of your nervous energy to make it work for you instead of against you.

Five ways of making Your Body Talk Powerful

How can you marshal your non-verbal tools – posture, gestures, body movements, facial expressions, and eye contact – and use them effectively when you speak? In this segment, you will learn five general methods to improve your body's spoken picture.

I.   Eliminate the Distractive Mannerisms

Dr. Ralph C. Smedley, the founder of Toastmasters International, said, "The speaker who sits and speaks at ease is the one who can be heard without uneasiness. If his stance and movements are so elegant and discrete that no one acknowledges them, he can be counted as genuinely useful. "If your acts are paired with your words, you will enhance the power of your expression – even though the listener does not explicitly hear them. But if your site activity includes mannerisms that are not linked to your spoken word, those behaviors will draw attention to themselves and away from your speech. In reality, rather than incorporating physical characteristics, an entrepreneur must also seek to eliminate impediments. What are the obstacles? You can usually detect at least a few visual disturbances in the delivery of each individual. Such mannerisms include the whole body, such as:

- Rocking out
- Swinging
- Moving

Such usually incompetent or unsuccessful speakers include:

- The grasping or leaning of the rostrum
- Tapping the thumbs
- Biting or kissing the mouth
- The shift in Jingling Pocket
- Scowling
- Hair or garment adjustment
- Switch the head and eyes from left to right like an oscillatory fan

Both of these acts share two things in common: first, they are physical expressions of essential nervousness; second, they are done unintentionally – the person is not sure that they are doing them. Many of us are mindful of our linguistic faults. But unless we have access to camera devices and monitor our gestures, many of our annoying mannerisms are unchallenged. The first step in removing unwanted mannerisms is to achieve a correct view of the spoken picture of your body. And you need guidance to do this. Your next move is to remove all physical activity that doesn't contribute to the voice. You will do this by being mindful of the problem areas and by conscious self-monitoring of future presentations. When you have a lot of problem areas, focus on one at a time. When each of them is eliminated, move on to the next.

II.   Be Normal, Informal, Conversational

The single most significant law to make the body talk efficiently is to be you. Today's popular speech style can better be represented as an amplified conversation. It's much more casual than the exquisite style that has dominated public speakers in years gone. Focus is focused on collaboration and exchange of thoughts – not on success or demonization. Don't want to mimic the next person. Instead, let yourself react instinctively and naturally to what you see, feel, and tell. Try to be as honest and familiar as when you speak to friends or family members.

III.   Let your body look at your emotions

A person under the influence of his emotions projects an authentic self, behaving

185

instinctively and spontaneously. If you're passionate about your subject, believe in what you're saying, and want to communicate your message with others, your physical gestures will come from inside and be relevant to what you're saying. By investing yourself in your letter, you can be intuitive and spontaneous without thinking about it.

IV.   Gain self-confidence through preparedness

Nothing affects the emotional outlook rather than the awareness that he or she is well trained. This awareness inspires self-confidence, a critical aspect of good public speaking. When you're well-prepared, your actions should be directed outward to your audience instead of internally to your anxieties. You will be less likely to give visual images that contradict what you think, and you will find it easier to be standard and intuitive. You can almost effortlessly project the beautiful characteristics of honesty, earnestness, and excitement. Train and rehearse the content before it becomes part of you, yet don't want to memorize the speech. This can defeat your preparation because the conscious effort you need to remember each word will make you nervous and tense. Instead, know the subject so well that you just need to memorize the chain of thoughts. You're going to see the words pop out randomly.

V.   Use your club as a laboratory for learning

Training is the secret to enhancing your results throughout every attempt. Your Toastmasters Club gives you a real classroom where you can gain useful experience. This is where errors cost you nothing, and the crowd is still polite, tolerant, and encouraging. Assist sessions diligently and talk as much as possible. Welcome input from your evaluators and listen closely to suggestions about the actions of the physical site. By integrating what you understand from this tutorial into your daily tasks, you will become adept at public speaking.

You're Speech Style

How you hold your body as you talk sends its collection of visual signals to the audience. Rather than anything else, it represents your mood, asking your listeners if you are calm, aware, and in charge of yourself and the speaking situation. A healthy speaking posture has other advantages for a speaker. It lets you breathe better and effectively project your voice. It also offers a reasonable starting point from which to make a gesture or move the body in some direction. And by making you feel both alert and relaxed, it helps relieve nervous anxiety and minimizes random, disruptive motions. What is the proper speaking posture? Tell someone else to read the next two paragraphs aloud while you follow the instructions:

Stand upright but not stiff, with the legs about six to 12 inches apart and slightly ahead. Balance your weight equally on your leg balls. Lean in for a little bit. Your legs are meant to be straight but not closed. Relax the shoulders, yet don't let them go. Keep your chest out and your back up. Your head should be erect and your chin up, but it's not that awkward. Let your arms hang naturally by your sides, your fingertips loosely bent. Now, take a couple of long, absolute breaths. If you feel relaxed? Your attitude should be sensitive, but not static, calm, but not messy. If this posture doesn't feel comfortable to you, consider repositioning your legs slightly, so your body feels relaxed. Do not hold the same role in the presentation. But if you move from one position to another, make a gesture, or shift your posture, be sure to align your body until your step is done.

Expressions

A gesture is an essential body expression that confirms a verbal statement or conveys a particular thought or emotion. Simultaneously, motions can be made with the head, shoulders, or legs, and thighs. Most of them are made with the hands and arms. Your hands can be great instruments of expression as you talk. But many novice speakers don't know what to do with their paws. Some people want to get them out of the way by putting them in their pockets or behind their backs. Others unintentionally alleviate emotional anxiety by making painful, disruptive gestures. A few performers over-gesture out of nervousness, shaking their arms and hands frantically. The movements of a speaker will provide a particular interpretation of the audience. The Indians of North America devised a sign language that would enable people with very separate spoken languages to converse. Sign language has made it easier for deaf people to communicate without speaking. The use of gestures in conversation differs from one society to another. In certain cultures, such as Southern Europe and the Middle East, people use their hands openly and expressively when they speak. In other countries, people use movements less often and are more subdued.

The essential gesture that we make and the significance that we bind to them are the results of our cultural experience. Just like cultures are distinct, so are the assumed meanings of gestures. For example, nodding one's head up and down means approval or permission in Western societies – but in certain parts of India, this gesture means the exact opposite. In certain parts of the world, a common symbol used in the United States that form a circle with a thumb and a forefinger to signify acceptance – is considered a provocation and an obscenity. To be successful, the movements of the speaker must be purposeful – even if they are done unintentionally. They ought to be clear to the public. They have to say the same thing to the listener as they do to the speaker. And they must represent what has been said, as well as the overall personality behind the post.

Why Gestures?

Many good speakers use actions. Why? Gestures are perhaps the most evocative type of non-verbal expression that a speaker may use. No other kind of physical movement will improve your voice in as many respects as your movements.

- Clarify your comments and help them. Gestures will enhance the audience's interpretation of your spoken word.

- Dramatize your thoughts, please. Along with what you mean, movements tend to build vibrant visions in the minds of your listeners.

- Give focus and energy to the spoken word. Gestures express your thoughts and attitudes more plainly than you speak.

- Give support to dissipate nervous energy. Purpose movements are a suitable medium for the nervous stress found in a speaking environment.

- Act as a visual aid. Gestures enhance the attention and retention of the audience.

- Stimulate the engagement of the group. Gestures will help you show the reaction you are expecting from your audience.

- Gestures offer visual help when you reach a broad group of people, and the whole crowd cannot notice your eyes.

Gesture Categories

Despite the significant number of movements that count as gestures, all gestures should be classified into one of the following main categories:

Descriptive expressions explain or reinforce spoken signals. They help the viewer understand similarities and parallels, and imagine the scale, form, motion, position, feature, and number of objects.

Emphatic expressions underscore what has been said. They point to earnestness and belief. For example, a clenched fist shows a positive emotion, such as rage or resolve.

Suggested movements are indicators of thoughts and feelings. They allow the speaker to establish the perfect mood or convey a specific opinion. An open palm typically means offering or accepting a view, while a shrug of the shoulders implies confusion, perplexity, or irony.

Prompting movements are used to help elicit the audience's desired reaction. If you want listeners to lift their hands, cheer, or take a particular action, you're going to improve the response by doing it yourself as an example.

Gestures made above the shoulder level indicate height, enthusiasm, or spiritual exultation. Gestures made below the story of the shoulder suggest denial, apathy, or condemnation. Those made at or above the status of the shoulder indicate calmness or serenity.

The most commonly used movements include an open palm kept forward to the viewer. The purpose of this kind of gesture depends on the location of the palm. Keeping the palm upward signifies offering or taking, even though this gesture is often seen as an unconscious action, with no clear intended purpose. A palm holding down can convey repression, confidentiality, completion, or stabilization. The palm holding out to the crowd indicates stopping, repulsion, rejection, or hatred. If the palm is placed perpendicular to the body of the speaker, it appears to show dimensions, space, or time constraints, parallels, or compares.

How to Treat Efficiently?

Gestures reflect the individual personality of each speaker. What's right for a speaker is not going to be for you. However, the following six principles apply to virtually anyone trying to become a creative, successful speaker.

1. React to, of course, what you hear, feel, and tell

When you make an expression, you instinctively express yourself by gestures. No matter what our attitude or cultural context may be, each of us has a strong tendency to punctuate and reinforce our words with gestures. The key is not to counteract the urge by hiding behind a mask of impassiveness; it will only produce a build-up of suspense. At the same time, don't make gestures from a book or another writer. Be yourself, really and instinctively. If you force unnatural movements on your natural style, your audience will notice it and call you a fake. Some are naturally animated, whereas others are naturally reserved. Use your hands openly when you talk informally, use them frankly when you chat. By default, you are a quiet, low-key guy, don't change your demeanor just to fit public speaking circumstances.

2. Establish the conditions of management

Your movements can be a mere outgrowth of your particular thoughts and emotions. They should emerge spontaneously and habitually from your approach to the message you are addressing. When you communicate, you're meant to be ultimately interested in talking – not worrying about your hands. The substance of the presentation must inspire your movements. By immersing yourself in your subject matter, you establish the conditions that will allow you to react spontaneously with appropriate actions.

3. Follow the term action and the occasion

Your visual and verbal signals must serve as collaborators in the expression of the same mind or thought. If a speaker struggles to fit words with gestures, the effect may be wooden, fake, and sometimes comical. Any gesture you make needs to be purposeful and representative of your comments. In this way, the audiences will recognize the result rather than the motion. Be sure that the vigor and strength of your movements are suitable for your phrases. Using powerful, emphatic gestures only when you sense the message is calling for them. You will need to change the activities to suit the scale and function of the audience on occasion. Generally speaking, the bigger the crowd, the broader and slower your actions should be. Bear in mind that young people are usually drawn to a speaker who uses aggressive motions. Still, older and more conservative groups may feel annoyed or intimidated by a speaker whose physical movements are too strong. The logistics of the speaking situation also influences your voice movements. When speaking from a physically constrained location, you can be prevented from using broad, sweeping motions. A typical example of a restricted speech role is the head table, where people sit next to the speaker.

4. Keep Your Actions Compelling

Your movements should be vibrant and distinct if they are to create the desired effect. A half-hearted motion suggests that the speaker lacks conviction and earnestness. A hand motion should be a whole-body movement starting from the shoulder – never from the elbow. Shift your whole arm out of your body comfortably and quickly. Hold the wrists and fingertips gentle, rather than rigid or tight. Efficient movements are energetic enough to be compelling and subtle sufficient to be broad enough. It's quickly apparent. Your actions should be distinct but not crazy, and they should never follow a fixed pattern.

5. Make the movements quick and time-consuming

Every single gesture has three parts: the approach, the stroke, and the return. Your body starts to turn in the expectation of the gesture during the procedure. The stroke is the action itself, and the return takes the body back to a relaxed speaking stance. The rhythm of a motion – focus, approach, stroke, recovery, balance – must be seamlessly performed in such a manner that only a stroke is noticeable to the viewer. Just as pacing is an integral aspect of comedy, the pace of a move is just as crucial as its consistency. The stroke must come with the right term – not before nor after it. However, the approach should be started long before the stroke; in fact, you should produce a particularly useful result by approaching the motion several seconds in advance and keeping the approach until the precise moment of the stroke. The return means keeping your hands on your sides smoothly – it doesn't have to be rushed. Don't want to memorize the expressions and blend them into the voice. Memorized gestures typically miss, since the speaker refers to the term that the gesture is intended to punctuate. This results in a motion that accompanies a phrase that seems fake and stupid.

6. Make natural, natural gesturing a habit

The first step in being adept at gesturing is to decide what you're doing right now. If you do, attempt to erase from the body's spoken portrait. Train to strengthen your movements – please don't delay for the day of your expression. Keep study to develop your gesturing capabilities in front of strangers, family members, and co-workers.

Relax your inhibitions, make a move when you feel like it, and let yourself respond instinctively to what you think, feel, and say. It would help if you made acceptable movements a part of your everyday actions through knowledge and practice.

Body movements

Body movement – shifting your position or location during the speech is the most comprehensive, most noticeable type of physical activity that you, as a speaker, can do. Because of this, it can be either a massive advantage or an enormous disadvantage for the distribution system. If you turn your whole body in a calm, purposeful manner during the speech, you will gain three ways. For instance, body movement will help and strengthen what you say. And, of course, the motion would almost always draw the interest of the viewer. Finally, using body movement is the quickest, most effective way of burning up nervous energy and alleviating physical stress. However, both of these features can have the ability to work against you. One law that makes body movement your partner, not your opponent, is this: never move without a cause. Inevitably, the mind is drawn to a moving target, so every movement of the body you make while speech attracts notice. Moving along with your verbal message for a cause enhances the alertness and attentiveness of the viewers while at the same time strengthening what you tell. Seeing a fixed object is tiring, so you don't want to hold to a particular spot when you're chatting. On the other side, your body's activity should be controlled by moderation.

So much body activity, for the right kind, can be disturbing to the audience. Ideally, you should pursue a middle ground that consists of enough action to hold your listeners' attention, but not enough to divert them away from what you're doing. And as purposeful gestures call for attention, so make spontaneous gestures. The body would do about anything to get rid of the stress. Inexperienced speakers typically execute body motions such as rocking, swaying, and pacing without being conscious of what they're doing. If public speaking makes you anxious and stressed, aim to integrate sufficiently purposeful body activity into your expression so that your body does not unintentionally engage in distracting mannerisms. Another good explanation for body activity is to increase the comprehension of your message. The forms suggested that several ways of body movement are less reliable than those caused by individual actions. Still, body movement can also be an essential visual complement to the spoken word.

Stepping ahead during a speech indicates that you have passed an important point. A move or two backward suggests that you have come to an end and can let the crowd rest for a moment and absorb what you've just learned. A lateral change means a transition – where you quit one mind and take another. In some instances, body movement may be used to demonstrate or dramatize a particular concept. E.g., whether you're explaining a physical event, such as tossing a ball, or a runner straining to smash the tape to win a close-up race, you can help your listeners better imagine what you're doing by acting out your explanation. The final answer for body movement is probably the simplest: to get from one position to another. In virtually any speaking case, you have to walk to and from the stage, and you give your message. And if you're adding visual aids into a presentation, you're going to switch around while you use them. The trick to successful movement is to make these movements fast, standard, and smooth. When changing your speaking posture during a sentence, always lead with the foot nearest your target. If you're going to jump to the side, take your left foot.

Facial Movement

Impassive speech can be an advantage for a successful poker player, but for a speaker, it is an obstacle to efficient communication. People are watching the speaker's face during the presentation. Politeness, of course, is one of the reasons for this. Still, equally significant is the desire to collect the visual evidence that would be made available to the speaker a more meaningful message. Facial language is also the primary determinant of the context of a word. Here's an indication of this. When a friend grinned warmly at you and said, "You're mad," would you feel insulted? Possibly not; in truth, you may even take it as a token of love. But what if a sneer of contempt followed this comment? Verbal communication would be the same, but there's no question that your answer will be profoundly different.

When you speak, your face expresses your behaviors, feelings, and desires more plainly than any other aspect of the body. According to behavioral psychology, people need to identify – by merely studying the facial expressions of the speaker – such distinct emotions as discomfort, anxiety, pleasure, uncertainty, resentment, curiosity, disbelief, rage, and sorrow. Your face acts as a barometer to the public on what's inside of you. Your audience will watch your face for hints about your honesty, approach to your message, and your earnestness in sharing your ideas with them. Erase gestures that don't apply on your lips. They involve irritating mannerisms and implicit gestures that are oblivious to the thoughts, behaviors, and emotions. Both forms of unnecessary facial expression are typically signing of nervousness. Just as nervous speakers display disturbing motions and body expressions, they can also release excess energy and anxiety by subtly shifting their facial muscles. Examples of spontaneous facial gestures involve chewing or clicking the tongue, twisting the jaw, lifting the corners of the mouth, and twitching motions on some part of the face.

The audience finds these gestures to be indicators of nervousness and loss of trust, knowledge, and readiness. Such behavior may also leave the audience uncomfortable and less receptive to the verbal communication of the speaker. When you know that you're showing disruptive facial gestures, work on managing your apprehensions about speaking. Detailed planning and participation with your subject matter would allow you to develop trust and influence. The trick to conveying friendliness is to try to smile. It's still unwise to do that – you could be branded as inconsequential, and it would be unacceptable to do that during a critical presentation. But, by all means, smile when it's necessary to the situation. Show your audience that you are happy to have the chance to share your thoughts with them, that you enjoy yourself and that you are interested in them. There are no laws regarding the use of particular terms. By releasing your inhibitions and encouraging yourself to react spontaneously to your feelings, behaviors, and emotions, your facial expressions would be acceptable, generating authenticity, confidence, and integrity.

Eye contact

Each of the categories we've just addressed physical appearance, stance, motions, body motions, and facial expressions contains essential non-verbal elements for your vocabulary. But after your voice, your eyes are your most effective contact weapon.

Why is communication with the eye essential?

When you talk, you engage your audience with your eyes and make your presentation clear, specific, and conversational. One sure way to sever the contact bond is not to glance at the target. No matter how big an audience can be, every listener needs to feel important, to feel intimate. Link to the speaker, and to believe that the speaker interacts personally with him or her. There's an amplified conversation. Much as a small, casual community feels disconnected from a discussion if the speaker doesn't reach his or her eyes, people in the crowd will feel cut out if you don't make eye contact with them. In most cultures, the act of staring at others squarely in the eye is a sign of honesty. Failure to hold another's eyes while communicating indicates disinterest, loss of faith, insincerity, or deception. The same social correlations can be observed in public speaking. In one analysis, those who developed eye contact were judged to be more accurate, trustworthy, reliable, polite, and skillful than those who did not.

Only by looking at your audience as individuals can you persuade them that you are serious, that you are interested in them, and that you care whether they support your message or not. Your eyes also act as a control system when you talk. Only by looking at them, you affect the focus and concentration of your audience. On the other side, if you don't look at them, they're not going to look at you, and you're going to suffer response to your word. In turn, the interest created by your good eye contact will serve as a source of strength and inspiration to you. When you see that your message is essential to the public, you will build trust and feel more relaxed. Eye communication will even help you conquer your nervousness. Fear is the most common source of anxiety in voice, and stress is caused by the unexpected. Eye interaction makes an amount transparent to the viewer. If you look at your audience and know that most of them are engaged in your message, your anxiety will evaporate, and the nervous stress will be minimized. Not only can your eyes transmit crucial signals when you're talking, but they're also still getting them.

Sufficient eye contact is an input system that renders the speech situation a two-way communicating operation. Only by looking at your listeners can you decide how they respond. Are you doing well? Will the listener get what you're talking about? Are you having the interest of the audience? Is your message accepted? By watching the responses of the crowd, you will make instant changes to the presentation. Experienced speakers believe this tactile input to be the best advantage of eye contact. If you have mastered the confidence to gauge the response of your audience and adapt your language accordingly, you can become a much more successful speaker.

How to use your eyes efficiently
1. Well, know your stuff

Preparing yourself maintaining the power of your verbal messaging is a requirement for creating successful eye contact with your audience. You should know your voice so well that you don't have to dedicate your mental resources to recalling the chain of thoughts and phrases. Your perception must be external to the viewer – not inward to inner chaos. If you can talk easily without words, do so by all means. But if you need to use an outline or any other sort of written reminder, go ahead. Just don't let it be a replacement for planning and rehearsal. You can use your eyes successfully when making notes, but it takes skill and deliberate effort. Many skilled speakers are incredibly competent at this practice, taking advantage of such regular breaks as the laughter of the crowd or the after-effects of an exciting topic to take a quick look at their notes. It would help if you kept your letters short a few essential words or symbols keyed to the order of your message to make this strategy effective. If you know the content and are well-prepared, these cues can be enough to keep you on track and prevent breaking eye contact with the audience.

Build a relationship with you. When you talk, you interact with a group of individuals, not acting in front of a single team. Efficient eye contact means more than just transferring your eyes around the room; it means reflecting on the individual listeners and establishing a person-to-person interaction with them. How are you doing this? Start by choosing an individual and talking to him or her directly. Keep the person's eyes long enough to create a conceptual bond, maybe five to ten seconds, or the time needed to utter a sentence or express a thought. Then shift your eyes to another guy. You may have observed a speaker waging his head from side to side, or slowly turning his attention from right to left like an oscillating fan. Often note that while your eyes ought to shift from one person to the next, they should not follow some pattern. For an audience of the size of a traditional Toastmasters club, this is reasonably easy to achieve. However, if you select one or two people in each part of the room and create personal relations with them, each audience can get the feeling that you're talking to him or her directly.

Visual input control

When you give a speech, your listeners respond with their non-verbal messages. Use your eyes to find this useful help. Through watching these visual signals, you will gauge the responses of the audience to what you say, and then change your layout accordingly. When people in the crowd are not smiling at you, they will not be listening to you either. It's often so you can't be heard when you don't have a microphone, sound loud to see if there's a good response. They might just be bored. If that is the case, you'll need to recover their attention, maybe by using acceptable language, increasing your vocal variation, or making some purposeful movements, or the body's motions. If you think the listeners are puzzled? If that is the case, you will need to have more clarity about what you said. Monitor them as you do, and when their faces register recognition, switch to the next stage or thought. Are your listeners frowning at you? Note the viewer is unintentionally mirroring the speaker. You might be unintentionally glaring at them. Smile and see how their gestures alter. The same holds for members of the crowd who are nervously fidgeting: you might have been disturbing physical mannerisms. On the other hand, if their expressions reflect joy, curiosity, and near attention, don't change it. You're doing a fine job.

How to make the first impression?

First experiences are somewhat meaningful. People meeting for the first time make instant assumptions on each other that permanently color their relationships. When you give a speech, you will be judged by the people in your audience, and the initial effect you deliver on them will significantly influence the performance of your presentation. One of your goals as a speaker is to create a visual picture that complements and strengthens your verbal message. You want your audience to respect you, to believe you, and to hear what you say. You have already made your first impression on your fellow club members as a Toastmaster. Know though, that your club is a learning workshop that trains you for outside speech offered to other people, and in the future, you will be presenting to business associations and the neighborhood. You're going to be a mystery to all of these viewers, and having a strong first impression would be significant.

Appearance matters a lot

Like it or not, your body image has a significant effect on how people evaluate you. When you give a speech, your presentation conveys a compelling visual message to the viewer that is crucial to your performance as a communicator. You can't change your age, height, or facial features so that you can improve your appearance through proper clothes, grooming, and exercise. This manual cannot contain extensive information on these subjects. The types and interests differ considerably over time, place, and socio-economic conditions. There are few common remarks for both speakers. A strict thumb rule for the dress is to be at least as well-dressed as the best-dressed person in the crowd. When your listeners are wearing suits and ties, eat the best case or dress to get you the most compliments. Make sure that every piece of clothing is tidy, well-tailored, and well-fitting. Don't wear jewelry that glitters or jingles when you're driving or make a motion. It could divert attention away from your voice. For the same purpose, clean your pockets of bulky items or stuff like pocket changes or keys that create audible sounds as you walk. Audiences want speakers representing mental health and physical vitality. Research has found that the listener correlates the well-being of a speaker with the soundness of his or her verbal messages. So, watch your diet and workout daily.

When you speak to the audience

Part of your first impression is made before you begin your voice. As the crowd enters, the plans should be finished. It would be best if you did not have to research the message. Instead, mix with the group and express the same fun, optimistic personality that will make the speech a success. Be attentive and courteous as the conference or curriculum starts. If you're anxious, relax gently and deeply. One speaker is advised to do isometrics. These unobtrusive training gestures go unnoticed by some and are useful for helping to dissipate nervous energy.

The first-minute importance

When you talk, mainly if you are not well known to the crowd, the most critical part of your performance is the first minute. In those few seconds, the people in the group are going to make important decisions about you. They will determine if you are confident, genuine, polite, willing to answer them, and deserving of their consideration. And to a large extent, they're going to base this decision on what they see. After your introduction, walk deliberately and steadily to your speaking role. Balance your body while you take your speaking part. Keep immediate interaction with the viewer, incorporating direct eye contact with a friendly smile. Keep your expressions and emotions to a minimum during the first few moments of your speech; let the crowd get used to you first.

Thumbs up on expressions

As speakers, we need to note that much of our message is not just in our voices, but also in our visual presentation. For some of us, this involves extending our expressions and facial gestures and cultivating a better understanding of eye touch. For some, it means modulating the very one's same characteristics as well. Whatever your physical strengths and communication skills, your ability to physically articulate your concepts through gestures and other modes of body language will improve not only your appearance but your overall success as a speaker.

CHAPTER 6: ROUTES TO THE CONVINCING, CORE, AND PERIPHERAL

The dominant trend of psychology over the last few decades has been that individuals do not necessarily work at their maximum mental potential. That is, often people think carefully about things, but they can't think carefully about every piece of knowledge or message they receive. Instead, people often rely on algorithms or shortcuts in decision-making. This differing degree of thinking or elaboration has repercussions about how evidence is obtained and its convincing effect. The ELM (Elaboration Likelihood Model) is an early example of what has been an eruption of dual-process and dual-system decision-making and assessment theories. However, rather than suggesting that people thought only in one manner or another, it presents a continuum of thought (elaboration). With different reasoning (or "route") taking place at either end of the continuum and a mixture of the respective techniques at either direction at a moderate level of thinking. Persuasion based on comparatively high degrees of thought is considered the critical path to influence. Whereas effectiveness, which happens with very little thought, is called the Peripheral way of convincing. These different routes mean that different people can respond to the same information very differently, or the same people can respond differently to the same information in other conditions. Importantly, whether persuasion emerges from comparatively high or low levels of thought can have somewhat different effects.

Primary Route

When inspired and willing to do so, people appear to closely examine the facts provided to them, analyzing the presumed core validity of the premises in the light of pre-existing expertise. Importantly, this improved thought does not immediately translate to an improvement in persuasion. An assertion (or piece of evidence) is only convincing if it gives rise to beneficial ideas in the receiver. A statement may be counterproductive to a persuasion effort if it is deemed to be wrong or, for the most part, causes unfavorable responses, such as counterarguments. Under the central path, the degree of change in mood depends on the importance of the thoughts generated in response to the message (favorable or unfavorable), the number of them, and how secure people are in their studies. The clearer thinking generated, the more confident it is, the more convincing it is. Since the central route depends on the assumed rather than the real nature of the main merits of the case, its persuasiveness will vary from person to person. It also means that high reasoning does not inherently amount to objectivity or fairness in judgment. Careful judgment may be impartial or may be skewed.

Peripheral route

Since people cannot give their full attention to every message, they are introduced. They frequently focus more on simplistic heuristics or peripherals, like the experience or popularity of the speaker or their current mood (e.g., "I liked that rally, so I must like that candidate"). In the political sense, a variety of reasonably necessary cues are available, which, in the absence of much thinking, may cause favorable judgments. The clearest example of this is the Democratic Party. Other powerful cues include likability, resemblance, and trust heuristics, including voting for someone because they seem likable, close to themselves, or trustworthy while not learning anything about the candidate's policies. Indeed, the essential assumed trustworthiness of the candidate's face has been shown to forecast election results. While simple cues, such as likability and confidence, often bring about improvement when people do not think much about the peripheral path, as will soon be discussed, these same simple cues may often affect attitudes through the central route.

Determinants of progress

If a message is interpreted through the central or peripheral route is determined by the degree of improvement it receives. Factors such as political engagement and expertise may decide the path to persuasion by influencing how often people are inspired or willing to learn about political messaging. In addition to information, the capacity to interpret a message may be affected by variables such as time constraints, obstacles, and the "channel" of communication. (self-paced media such as written materials are more straightforward to interpret than audio or video, the speed of which is fixed in production). In addition to political interest, motivational considerations influencing the amount of thought include such aspects as to how the receiver finds the subject to be individually significant, whether there is any perceived standard of appraisal (i.e., accountability), as well as some personality distinctions. Three characteristics that are extremely important and have generated a great deal of attention are the need for cognition (how much someone likes to consider and solve problems). The need to analyze (how much someone wants to assess things and make firm decisions on concepts). And the need for clarity (how much someone likes to get a prompt answer).

Elaboration implications

As factors enhance the probability of reasoning by increasing one's motivation or skill, essential signals become less critical determinants in attitudes, while meaningful roles and claims become more acute. Since political material (and one's reaction to it) is more closely evaluated in the sense of improved planning, this information is more likely to be adequately incorporated into the pre-existing mental structure of the recipient for assessment. Behaviors formed or modified by the central route are more expected to be stronger and more significant than the same attitudes developed or altered peripherally. This implies that actions in a prominent way would be more accessible (come to mind quickly), more optimistic (seen to be more legitimate), more consistent over time. Thus, while the two paths of influence can lead to what seems like the same mindset, they can have very different and significant implications? Next, we can see how the same variable can lead to convincing by either the central or the peripheral path.

Several functions

To date, we have noted two ELM (elaboration likelihood model) claims. Two simple convincing routes function at the end of the elaboration spectrum and vary in related issues. They consider necessary to result in a change of attitude; and while both routes may result in straightforwardly similar outcomes, the primary way of persuasion, with its more elaborate processing, results in a strong one.

How better you react to body language?

Depending on Your Personality Style Body Language is a big part of your conversation, but certain people don't pay enough attention to it. Here's how you react to body language, depending on your form of personality.

INFJ:

INFJs are sensitive people who pay attention to their environment. They pay attention to the descriptions and attitudes of people, which is why they can interpret them so well. INFJs will identify those actions in body language and can use them to help understand others and what they experience. INFJs are in contact with other people's feelings, and while verbal responses are a bit part of how others perceive each other, their body language is much more critical. INFJs are also not the most articulate individuals, which is why others must be able to pick up body language.

ENFJ:

The ENFJs are undoubtedly fantastic at interpreting body language, which is why they are so good at reading the feelings of others. Although ENFJs pay attention to what people think, they spend much more attention to their body language. They know that the way people act emotionally will sometimes reflect how they feel a lot more than what they think. Body language is essential to ENFJs, and they naturally can identify people's physical indices.

INFP:

INFPs are socially isolated people, but they sometimes tend to take a look back instead of getting to the middle of the thing. This will help them pick up the signals that other people are communicating with themselves. They positively respond to body language, but they don't like to pull, either. They want to provide people space, which is why they are not continually paying close attention to the inner feelings of others. INFPs would like to let people show themselves as they can do so.

ENFP:

ENFPs consider the body language of others, even though they do not make this explicit on their own. They don't want people to know how much they pick up and love giving people rights. They will pay attention to people's actions and lock it up if they need the detail later. ENFPs like to reflect on their freedom and do not want to linger or smother people with their thoughts.

INTJ:

INTJs always tend to pay attention to as much information as they can acquire, but only when it appears to be relevant. INTJs should not often pay careful attention to the body language of other people, since they may not understand. They don't like trying to read into the tiniest aspects of someone else's actions, so they want people to be upfront and honest. If for some other reason, the INTJ feels it is relevant, they will take the time to find out what's going on with that person. INTJs are perhaps not the most articulate people themselves, so body language can be the only way to interpret their actions or emotions.

ENTJ:

ENTJs are more focused on paying attention to their ambitions and working on getting something done. They like to reflect on their interests and obligations, and they don't like having to pay close attention to the feelings of others. The ENTJ must retain a sense of space from those around them and enjoy freedom. ENTJs are not effective at understanding people, and they tend not to pay constant attention to their actions because they are someone they care deeply for.

INTP:

INTPs will undoubtedly continue to pay careful attention to details and sometimes want to interpret body language rather than verbal answers. INTPs know that not all people say is what they think. They are well aware that body language is an essential way of communicating oneself, and they will undoubtedly attempt to read it in others. They're certainly trying to pay careful attention to the body language of the people around them to get a better reading of their actions. INTPs are just not excellent at interpreting feelings because what they pick up will be difficult for them to handle.

ENTP:

ENTPs certainly know that body language is an integral aspect of the comprehension of others. They're likely to pay careful attention to someone's actual behavior as they learn to read them correctly. Although ENTPs may pick up on body language and attempt to better interpret someone's actions in this manner, they can lack understanding of their emotions. It may be difficult for them to process what they see in that person because feelings are not always their strong suit.

ISTJ:

ISTJs aren't efficient in reading body language, so they want people to be upfront on what they want. They're not fans of trying to dig further, so reading thoughts can be challenging for them. The ISTJs want the people around them to be transparent and frank with them about what they want and what they believe. This way, the ISTJ will find a realistic solution to any dilemma that the individual is having. For the ISTJs, getting to pick up on hidden clues is not exactly their most vital point.

ESTJ:

ESTJs are certainly not fond of trying to pick up on body language and more apparent habits. They'd rather be with independent people and upfront with their desires. If someone is frustrated or in need of help, the

ESTJ needs the person to make things understandable to them without holding back. People who continually need others to translate their body language may be incredibly irritated and puzzled by the ESTJ.

ISFJ:

ISFJs are compassionate people who like to pay careful attention to the needs of those around them. The ISFJs understand the value of body language and will undoubtedly pay careful attention to it. They know that collecting the physical actions of the people around them can allow them to consider what they experience. People don't show themselves honestly, and their body language will give away what they feel.

ESFJ:

The ESFJs adapts well to body language and take time to understand the physical reactions of others. The ESFJs also do this instinctively, which allows them to understand the feelings of those around them. The ESFJs are in touch with the emotions of others and are profoundly concerned about the wishes of their loved ones. Because of this relationship with the feelings of people, the ESFJs pay particular attention to their body language to understand what they experience and not merely what they verbalize to others.

ISTP:

The ISTPs just don't pay much attention to the feelings of others, so they tend to preserve a sense of individuality. They don't like trying to pick up on the overt actions of someone, and they like people that are upfront on what they want. ISTPs are physical beings, but they understand when people have different physical reactions. They're just not great at deciphering feelings, which makes it impossible to bring things together.

ESTP:

ESTPs certainly understand that someone shows a different body language than usual. They know when someone doesn't respond to them the way they usually do, and they will react to it. They may become very depressed if their loved ones begin to be emotionally distant, as ESTPs are closely linked to the physical world around them. They will naturally be conscious of the material changes in others, and they will want to react accordingly.

ISFP:

The ISFPs note the body language and subtle variations in people's physical actions. They like, however, when people can articulate themselves freely because interpreting these signals can feel intrusive. The ISFPs want their loved ones to be upfront and frank with them, and to share their emotions more freely.

ESFP:

The ESFPs also understand body language better than anything else, since they are in touch with the real world around them. They will also note that someone behaves weirdly or not feeling right, purely based on their body language and outward appearances. For ESFPs, it is often better to understand people based on how they express themselves visually than verbally.

CHAPTER 7: ART OF PERSUASION

A persuasion is an act of persuading others to change their views or to do what you say. Influence has always been represented as a delicate type of art, but what makes it so healthy? Understanding the art of persuasion cannot only help you know how to manipulate people; it can also make you more aware of the strategies that you may use to try to alter your values and attitudes.

Is persuasion an art, and why?

To understand the art of persuasion, you must first understand the broader meaning of philosophy. Art is a method and a commodity that:

- Expresses intense feelings
- Intellectually demanding
- Complex and consistent
- Conveys confusing signals
- Shows a single point of view
- Produces an entity or output that involves a high level of ability

It is still clear how many of the above characteristics refer to types of art such as painting and playing music; they do not all refer to the art of convincing. Persuasion is not an art form in the same way as painting or music but instead includes highly tuned artistic skills-or the art-of language and conversation. However, persuasion does contain some of the characteristics of more conventional types of painting. It's mentally demanding, challenging, articulate, and loyal to your character.

What is the point of persuasiveness?

You may consider why you should want to learn how to impress others. You may also think that such a "craft" is diabolical or deceptive. The reality, though, is that any successful person has been able to convince others of something at one time or another. For example, most people have to ask the boss to hire them before they can even start working and making money. Persuasion is moving to several humanitarian efforts. Salespeople convince customers to purchase goods or services. Politics are persuading voters to help and vote for them. Con artists are persuading people to fall for scams and waste money they don't have. You may convince your teacher to take a makeup exam, encourage your girlfriend or partner to marry you or persuade others to assist with your service program. It's pretty hard to find people getting something done without any sort of persuasion. So, it's just not a matter of whether you can practice better methods of convincing. The concern is that you haven't already done it.

Factors to be considered in the art of convincing

All should learn the art of convincing. It needs determination to know how to do it successfully. Some people seem to have the ability to persuade people to see it that way. If you find it hard to remember, it's not the end of life. You can and will learn how to master this kind of craft. Here are several things to remember when you decide to convince someone:

Evaluate how simple the convincing can be

You should begin by feeling how difficult it is to win over the audience. Researchers have described many influences that affect how easy it can be to persuade others of something. All you need to do is follow the correct instructions and strategies.

Group member

When you are a member of a group, you are objectively less likely to be convinced of topics or ideas that run contrary to the opinions to your fellow group members.

Low self-esteem

People with low self-esteem are significantly much more comfortable to persuade than people with higher self-esteem. This is more likely because they appear to trust the views of others more than they do their own. The biggest obstacle you're going to face here is to assess the level of self-esteem of the person you're trying to convince. You will also do this by examining variables such as body posture, voice confidence, and dedication to the audience's point of view.

Inhibiting aggression

If you don't want to display confrontation, you're more likely to be surpassed by a smooth talker fluent in persuasion. And if they make you feel dissatisfied with something, they're trying to persuade you of, lack of provocation will make it easy for them to manipulate your decisions. People who are not inclined to violence don't argue what the other person suggests.

Depression and anxiety behaviors

Research suggests that unhappy people are more readily persuaded to accept someone else's opinions on their own. This is primarily attributed to factors such as lack of violence and self-esteem, as described above. However, you can find that certain people who suffer from depression will not be convinced by you, but rather cooperate with you to prevent confrontation.

Social inferiority

Many of those who think themselves socially insufficient appear to be more readily convinced. Even if they are no more socially incompetent than most, the fact that they perceive themselves in this manner causes them to put the responsibility of interaction on the person they communicate with. This makes it easy for the person to reassure them without being challenged.

How to Practice Persuasiveness?

Get the Appropriate Introduction

It's incredibly difficult to persuade an outsider of something. For example, salespeople dislike cold calling because they never know the kind of person they're dealing with on the other hand. They don't know their beliefs, interests, or whether they belong to a party that rejects what / how they're offering. Just as essential, the person calling does not know, and the salesperson does not trust. If you can get an introduction from a mutual friend or colleague, you have a lot better chance of persuading others to consider your perspective. If you can't find an opening, it allows you ready for something before you try to convince yourself. This is where outstanding listening and leadership skills come into the frame.

Worth of the hearing

When you first listen, you collect the details you need to build a customized presentation that makes sense to the person you're trying to convince. Skilled election candidates don't just turn up at the door and start to read. Instead, they usually ask a few questions about your beliefs to reach a starting point for their persuasion. In addition to the knowledge you get from listening, you build the feeling that you trust the other person and agree with their views.

On the other hand, they are more inclined to shape a complementary view of you and listen to what you have to say.

When you don't believe, be respectful

It's important to discuss your consensus with the person you're trying to reassure as much as possible. This shows that you value them and that you are broad-minded. Everyone needs to be thought of as wise because if you're going to contradict anything anyone does, they're just going to ignore you. Of course, on anything, you can't compromise with anybody, nor should you have to. Although you did, you wouldn't have been able to persuade your group to change their stance. You should maintain a kind approach that respects the rationale behind what they believe and the decisions they make.

Subtlety is essential

If you can say precisely what you want someone to believe, and they think it right away, there's not much need for convincing. More often than not, you ought to convince them in positive ways that your point of view is right. There are several different ways of convincing to be used, but the most powerful are those that are not obvious or apparent. Instead, they are based on making associations, sharing stories, and understanding the other person and where they stand.

Persuasion and Values

The art of convincing involves persistence and dedication to the method. If it were a matter of just saying, "Believe me!" there wouldn't be a lot of justification involved. You ought to take the time to formulate your points and justify your logic, implicitly, and consistently, to change someone's mind. If it's a short letter, it does not take a long time to send. But if you want to express anything more complicated, you need to be careful and engage with your audience.

Whose opinion matters?

If you bring your argument to a close, you can represent your conclusion as entirely right. However, people are more quickly convinced if they feel that they are coming to their judgment. They like to think that they decide to change their views, values, or behavior. The good news is, if you put out your point in a manner that makes sense to your viewers, they're likely to believe that their change of mind was their own choice. They would also be more likely to continue to hang on to that belief and, most critically, to act on it.

Legal issues

There are a few legal dilemmas to examine if you intend to learn the art of convincing. Many individuals have mischievously used manipulation methods to harm or take advantage of others. Before you decide to persuade others to work with you, think about the effect they will have if you succeed.

Undue interference

Undue interference is a legal concept that implies that you persuade others to behave according to their own free choice, without regard to the consequences. This becomes a matter of interest because someone is affected in a way and unable to make their own choices. For example, a caregiver may persuade an elderly adult to change their will and leave it. If you suggest studying the practice of persuasion, it is a spiritual necessity to resist excessive control. It'll keep you out of legal trouble too.

Misrepresenting statements

If you're in court or making a social media post, it's unethical to make misleading claims, papers, or pictures to support your case. If you wish to be responsible and considerate in your practice of convincing, you need to make sure that the facts or keeping information you give are reliable and valid to the best of your ability.

Perpetual Scams

People who use their convincing fluency to scam others don't care if what they do is harming someone. Sometimes, the people they end up persuading try to convince others of the same stuff without realizing that they were conned. It is essential to keep the facts straight and alert to the potential of deceit.

Is convincing positive or negative?

Just like every other type of practice, persuasion is neither positive nor negative in itself. It is how you use the art of influence, and for what reason, that decides whether you are adding something valuable to the world. The failure to impress others can be a considerable handicap in life. You may have problems finding a job, buying a house, or taking the next step in your relationship. On the other hand, you might find that you are so easily swayed and fall for any trick you have been faced with. If so, there are various ways to reduce the vulnerability to falling because of any slick come-on. A therapist will help you develop your self-esteem, strengthen your life skills, and learn how to handle your depression.

These variables are going to make you less vulnerable to deceit.

Secrets of persuasive people

If you encourage your boss to finance your initiative or your preschooler to wipe away his tush after using the toilet, convincing is an ability that is integral to your progress in life. Persuasive people have an uncanny tendency to make you lean toward their way of thought. Their hidden weapon is the possibility. They're trying to get you to like more than their ideas; they're going to get you to like them.

Here are the 15 trading tricks that incredibly convincing people use to their benefit.

1. They know about their audience

Persuasive people know their listeners inside and outside, and they use this information to express the language of their listeners. If it's toning down your aggressiveness when talking to someone who's reserved or churning it up with an angry, high-energy sort, everyone is different, and keeping up on these subtleties is a long way to getting them to hear your perspective.

2. They connect with the audience

People are much more likely to consider what you have to say because they feel what kind of person you are. In a negotiating report, Stanford students were asked to agree in class. Without some sort of training, 55 percent of students have successfully reached an agreement. However, when students were told to identify themselves and discuss their history before seeking to reach an agreement, 90 % did so effectively. The objective here is to stop getting too entangled in the back and forth of the conversation. The person you're talking to is a person, not a competitor or a target. No matter how exact the point is, if you don't communicate on a personal basis, he or she will doubt anything you say.

3. They don't push others

Persuasive people develop their ideas confidently and enthusiastically, without being hostile or violent. Pushy people are a drastic shift. The in-your-face technique begins with the receiver backpedaling, and they're heading for the hills before long. Persuasive people don't demand anything, and they don't require vigorously for their role because they realize that the subtlety is what wins people over in the long run. If you want to be more hostile, concentrate on being optimistic yet relaxed. Don't be anxious and stubborn. Know that if you genuinely have a good idea, people can catch on if you give them time. If you don't, they're not going to catch on at all.

4. They're not the mousy

From the other side, delivering the concepts as questions or as if they required validation makes them seem to be incomplete and unconvincing. If you seem to be quiet, concentrate on expressing your thoughts as claims and fascinating information to the other person. Also, exclude the qualifiers from your speech. When you're striving to be compelling, there's no room for "I guess" or "It's likely."

5. Using constructive body language

Becoming familiar with your movements, expressions, and tone of voice (and making sure they are positive) will attract people and open them to your points. Using an enthusiast accent, uncrossing your arms, keeping eye contact, and moving into the person who speaks is supportive body language that convincing people use to impress others. Strong body language will motivate the audience and persuade them that what you say is true. When it comes to compelling how you say things may be more important than what you say.

6. They are both straightforward and precise

Persuasive people can express their thoughts quickly and simply. When you have a good understanding of what you're talking about, it's fun and straightforward to explain to those who don't understand. The right approach here is to know the subject so that you can describe it to a child. If you can easily justify yourself to someone who has no experience on the subject, you can make a convincing argument for someone who does.

7. They are real and honest

Being real and genuine is essential for us to be persuasive. No one ever likes a fake. People gravitate to others who are sincere, and they feel they can trust them. It's hard to accept someone when you don't know who they indeed are and how they think. Persuasive people are mindful of who they are. They are happy enough to be relaxed in their skin. By reflecting on what inspires you and makes you comfortable as an entity, you become a far more engaging and convincing person than if you try to win people over by pretending to be the person, they want you to be.

8. They consider your point of view

The argument is an incredibly useful technique of persuasion. Please accept that your claim is not good. This indicates that you are open-minded and able to make changes instead of arrogantly sticking to your cause. You want your viewers to know that their best interests are at your heart. Consider using comments like, "I see where you're coming from," and, "It makes a lot of sense." This shows that you're listening to what they're saying. And you're not merely trying to push your thoughts on them. Persuasive people encourage others to be entitled to their views, and they accept personal views as genuine. They do this because it displays appreciation, making the other person more inclined to consider their perspective.

9. They ask good questions

The most significant mistake people have when it comes to listening is not hearing what they're saying, so they're focused on what they're going to say next, or how the other person is going to influence them. Words come out loud and straightforward, but the sense is lost. An easy way to prevent it is to ask a lot of questions. People want to hear that you're listening because anything as fundamental as a clarification question demonstrates not just that you're listening, but also that you care about what they're saying. You'll be shocked by how much appreciation and respect you receive from raising questions.

10.   Visual presentations

Research indicates that audiences are far more likely to be influenced by something that has graphics that carry it to life. Persuasive people use strong graphic representations to focus on this. Real photographs are not accessible or necessary; they tell vibrant storylines that breathe life into their ideas. Good tales create memories in the minds of recipients that are easy to connect to and hard to forget.

11.   They leave a positive first impression

Research suggests that most people decide whether they want you in the first seven seconds of the meeting. Then they spend the remainder of the discussion mentally explaining their initial response. This can sound scary, but by understanding this, you will take advantage of it to make substantial progress in your resilience and willingness to convince. Initial experiences are intimately related to constructive body language. Strong expression, a firm handshake, a smile, and opening your arms to the person you're talking to would help guarantee that your first impression is a positive one.

12.   They know how to stand in front of audiences

Insistence is a direct challenge of persuasion, so move softly when you want to convince people to decide immediately, finding demonstrated that they are often more likely to endorse their original view. Your impatience leads them to fight your points for their own sake. If your place is right, you're not meant to be scared to back off and give it time to sink in. Good ideas are always challenging to process immediately, and a little effort will go a long way.

13.   They recognize people by name

Your name is a vital part of your personality, and it sounds terrific when people use it. Persuasive people make sure they use the names of others any time they meet them. You're not supposed to use someone's name when you meet him or her. Research indicates that people feel valued when the person they're referring to speaks to them by name. If you're brilliant with faces but have difficulty with words, have fun with them and making people remember their names a brain exercise. When you meet people, don't be scared to ask for their name a second time if you forget it right after you hear it. You're going to have to keep the word handy, so you remember next time you see the person.

14.   They are pleasers

Persuasive people never fight a battle only to lose a war. They know how and when to hold their ground, but they are continually making sacrifices to support their cause. They still give in, give land, and do things to those that make them happy. Persuasive people do this, and they know that this won people over in the long term. They know that it's easier to be good than to be "right."

15.   They always keep smiling

People usually (and unconsciously) reflect the body language of the person they are referring to. If you want people to respect you and trust in you, smile at them during a conversation, and, as a result, they will automatically return the favor and feel happy. Persuasive people laugh a lot, and they have a real passion for their ideas. This has a cumulative effect on all the people they meet.

How to read and persuade people with six robust courtroom techniques?

Recognize the 'three personality positions'

Image of three chairs lined up in a row. The first chair is your public face, the way you want to look to everyone. The second is your secret face, the feelings of inadequacy that you keep hidden or only share with your friends. The third is your hidden identity, the thing that motivates you to make fake fronts, for example, something that happened to you as a teenager. Start by reflecting on someone's first chair in an initial conversation. Encourage them to chat about what they think is fascinating. Let them show their greatness, and they'll be flattered that you're involved in building confidence.

Understand and sympathize

To link to a deeper level, speak to your second chair next. Place yourself in the hands of the other person: consider how they feel and talk about those feelings. You don't even have to ask questions; just make observations. For instance, you might say, "It must be a struggle to run your own company with so many people dependent on you." So shut up, listen, and let them express themselves. You know, when you respect their role, it shows them that you see them. Be kind and speak to the person's heart. If you're not sure how they think, share the analogies of your life and see how they align with them.

Be honest

You have to talk from your own to someone's third chair. Conversely, to what we're sometimes instructed, it's all right to express your feelings about communicating with others. Being vulnerable to your insecurities or worries is the perfect way to create confidence and allow others to open up. When we start a courtroom, we first tell the jurors what we fear the opposing side will do. For example, if our client were prosecuting a dishonest business associate, we could suggest to the jury, "You should sure the prosecution can tell you that our client wasn't affected by this crime because he's wealthy and prosperous." When they hear that, the jury would think, "We're not going to fall for that."

Focus on body language and voice tone

"Mirroring" is a common practice where you unconsciously imitate the pose of the other person, such as leaning back or avoiding eye contact. You may sense how someone feels by watching their body language and listening to their speech. Does it sound familiar and fit with what they say? For example, if their words represent confidence, but they cannot meet your eyes, they may lack confidence. Focus on their facial gestures and glance at their eyes. We shake hands with every member of the jury by eye contact, focusing on someone until we see their head turn subtly, signaling that we are related to them. Be mindful in your voice, including your accent and intonation. For example, you might lower your voice to establish a sense of intimacy and deliberately pause to lead a discussion.

Address your objections

Through power and justification, you may counter the preconceived objections, statements, and prejudices of the other individual. That's why we ask the jury early in the trial to uncover all their biases to fix them. E.g., "Some people believe like wealthy business owners don't deserve the significant awards we're aiming for. Can you feel like that? "Listen to them and thank them for expressing their viewpoint. To resolve objections, do not undermine their beliefs; only encourage them to be open to your point of view, reframe the issue, and answer their concerns. Describe what you should do with them instead of selling them. Paint an idea of what their life would be like if they knew of what you were offering. Ask them to explain their experiences in detail despite their current problems, using the five senses and the present tense.

Principles of persuasion

Why is it that some people are so highly persuasive? Should we all take advantage of those abilities? After researching the most influential political, educational, business, and religious figures and testing countless strategies out of me, these are the 21 crucial lessons that I've found for persuading people.

1. Persuasion is not manipulation

Manipulation is intimidation by pressure to get others to do something that is not in their interests. Persuasion is the art of convincing people to do things that are in their best part and help you.

2. Convince the Persuadable

Everybody can be convinced, with the correct time and meaning, but not always in the short term. Democratic candidates spend their time and money on a limited collection of swinging electors who plan to vote. The first step in persuasion is often to recognize specific individuals who are convincing to your point of view at a given moment and to concentrate your energies and attention on them.

3. Timing and Context

Context and pace are the fundamental building blocks of persuasion. Context provides a clear norm of what is appropriate. For example, the Experiment has demonstrated that overachieving students could be shaped into dictatorial correctional officers. Timing determines what we expect from people and our lives. We choose to marry a different sort of person than we do when we're younger because what we want is a transition.

4. You've to be involved in being convinced

You will never convince someone who isn't interested in what you're saying. We are always most interested in ourselves, and we spend most of our time worrying about the future, love, or health. The first art of convincing is learning how to speak to people about them all the time; if you do that, you'll have their captive interest.

5. Cooperation obligates

When someone do something for you, you feel obligated to do something for him or her. It's part of our evolutionary DNA to help each other survive as a community. More specifically, you can unduly exploit reciprocity in your favor. By making small gestures of kindness to others, you will ask for more back in exchange, which they would gladly give.

6. The Consistency in a work

The person who can continue to question what they want, and who continues to show importance, is essentially the most convincing. The way too many historical personalities have eventually convinced millions of people to remain vigilant in their actions and message. Remember Abraham Lincoln, who lost his mother, three sons, his sister, his spouse, fell in business and lost eight consecutive elections before he was appointed president of the United States.

7. Perfectly complement

We are also profoundly influenced by compliments, and we are more likely to trust people with whom we have positive feelings. Try to congratulate others honestly and sometimes on something they're not generally complimented with. It's the best thing you can do to convince someone that costs nothing but a moment of contemplation.

8. Place your objectives

A lot of persuasions are balancing the desires of others to trust your decision. The CEO who guarantees a 20 percent rise in revenue and a 30 percent increase is rewarded, while the same CEO who offers a 40 percent increase and produces 35 percent is fined. Persuasion is essentially about knowing and over-expecting the perceptions of others.

9. Don't presume

Don't ever think about what someone wants; only show your worth. We often avoid selling our products/services because we feel that others don't have the money or interest. Don't guess what someone will or may not want, give what you can, and leave the decision.

10.   Build your scarcity

Apart from the need to live, nearly everything has a perceived meaning. We like things because these things are what other people like. If you want somebody to want what you've got, you've found ways to make the item scarce, even though it's yourself.

11.   Build Emergency

You ought to be able to induce a sense of urgency in people who want to move right away. If we're not inspired enough to do anything right now, we're unlikely to have any incentive in the future. We have to reassure people, and desperation is our most important card to play.

12.   Graphics matters a lot

What we see is more effective than what we hear. That could be why pharma firms are now so close to the potentially terrible side effects of their medications as they set the backdrop for people watching the sunset in Hawaii. Your first thoughts are perfect. And master the ability to build a picture for others, the vision of their eyes, of a potential event that you will have for them.

13.   Tell the truth

Often the most powerful way to reassure someone is to teach them things about themselves that nobody else can admit. Faced with harsh facts are the most prevalent, essential incidents that have taken place in our lives. Truth-tell without bias or agenda, and you will also find the responses of others fascinating.

14.   Develop a relationship

This applies to our unconscious actions outside our deliberate decisions. By mirroring and balancing other regular habits (body language, intonation, voice rhythms, etc.), you will create a sense of relationship where people are more relaxed with you and are more open to your ideas.

15.   Flexibility of actions

It's the most versatile, not necessarily the strongest, who's in charge. Children are also compelling that they tend to go through a litany of actions to get what they want (pouting, screaming, negotiating, begging, and charming), while adults are left with a simple "no" answer. The greater the collection of actions, the more compelling you would be.

16.   Learn how to pass energy

Some people strip our energy away from us, and others infuse us with it. The most successful people know how to shift their motivation to others, inspire, and invigorate them. It's often as simple as eye contact, body interaction, humor, interest in verbal response, or even active listening.

17.   Communicate clearly and effectively

If you can't describe the idea or point of view to an 8th grader in such a manner that they can tell it to another adult with ample clarification, it's too hard. The art of convincing is to simplify everything down to its heart and explain to people what they truly care about.

18.   Being organized give you the edge

Your starting point ought to be to know something about the people and circumstances around you. Planning and preparation facilitate a successful argument. For example, in a work interview, you significantly boost the chances of being well versed in the company's goods, programs, and history.

19.   Keep calm and isolate in confrontation

Nobody is more successful when they are "On Tilt." In conditions with remarkable ability, you will still have the most influence through remaining relaxed, detached, and compassionate.

20.   Use frustration for intent

Many of the people are unhappy with the confrontation. Whether you're able to intensify the situation to a heightened level of uncertainty and conflict, in certain conditions, some will come back down. Using this sparingly, and should not do so from an irrational point of view or lack of self-control. But note, you can use rage purposefully to your benefit.

21.   Conviction and self-assurance

Performance is not as persuasive, intoxicating, and desirable as certainty. It is the one who has an unbridled sense of confidence that will always convince others. When you genuinely believe in what you're doing, you're still going to inspire people to do what's best for them while getting what you want in exchange.

Psychological convincing strategies

Every day, we are faced with persuasion in a wide range of ways. The average citizen is subject to thousands of advertisements a day. Meat producers want us to purchase their newest items, while film companies want us to watch the next blockbusters. Since manipulation is such a ubiquitous aspect of our lives, it is also all-too-easy to forget how we are affected by outside sources. Persuasion is not simply helpful to advertisers and salespeople. Learning how to use these methods in your day-to-day life will help you become a successful negotiator and make it more realistic that you'll get what you want, whether you're trying to persuade your baby to eat her vegetables or to force your employer to grant you the bonus. Since persuasion is so effective in so many areas of everyday life, the strategies of persuasion have been practiced and experienced since ancient times. It wasn't until the beginning of the 20th century, though, that social scientists started to research these effective strategies systematically.

Main Persuasion Strategies

The end aim of convincing is to persuade the target to internalize the convincing claim and to accept this new mindset as part of their core value system. The below are only a handful of the most powerful means of convincing. Other approaches include the use of incentives, penalties, constructive or negative expertise, and many others.

Trying to create a need

One form of convincing requires the development of a desire or an appeal to an established desire. This kind of persuasion relates to a person's simple needs for shelter, affection, self-esteem, and self-actualization. Marketers often use this tactic for marketing their goods. Remember, for example, how many commercials indicate that people choose to buy a certain product to be satisfied, healthy, loved, or appreciated.

Adjust to societal needs

Another very successful persuasion tactic is appealing to the desire to be famous, respectable, or equivalent to others. Television advertisements include many examples of this form of manipulation, in which audiences are persuaded to buy products so that they can be like someone else or be like a well-known or admired individual. Television ads are a huge source of convincing publicity.

Use words and pictures

Persuasion sometimes uses filled words and images. Advertisers are well conscious of the influence of encouraging terms, which is why so many advertisers use expressions such as "Fresh and improved" or "All Natural."

Put your foot on the doorstep

Another method that is also useful at getting people to comply with the order is known as the "foot-in-door" strategy. This persuasive technique entails getting a person to commit to a specific request, such as asking them to buy a small object, followed by a much larger request. By getting the person to consider the tiny initial favor, the claimant already has his "foot in the door," making the recipient more likely to cooperate with the larger offer. For instance, a neighbor wants you to take care of her two children for an hour or two. After you commit to a lesser offer, she wonders if you would only take care of the children for the remainder of the day. Since you have already committed to a specific request, you might feel obligated to consider a larger request. This is a clear example of what psychologists refer to as the law of loyalty, and advertisers also employ this tactic to persuade customers to purchase goods and services.

Go large, then little

This strategy is the reverse of a foot-to-door strategy. A seller may begin by making a big, frequently impractical request. The person responds by refusing to sell, figuratively closing the door. The salesperson answers by making a much smaller offer, which sometimes tends to be conciliatory. People always feel they pressured to respond to these deals. Since they rejected the original offer, people always feel obligated to support the vendor by approving a smaller appeal.

Use the force of mutual support

If people do you a favor, you typically have an almost irresistible responsibility to return the favor in kind. This is regarded as the practice of reciprocity, a social duty to do something for someone else because they did something for you first. Marketers may take advantage of this propensity by making it seem that they are giving you good, such as providing "extras" or discounts, and would force customers to consider a deal and make a purchase.

Establish an anchor point for your corporation

The anchoring bias is a subtle cognitive bias that can have a strong effect on agreements and decisions. To make a compromise, the first bid appears to become a focal point on all future discussions. So, if you're trying to negotiate a pay rise, being the first one to propose an amount, particularly if that amount is a little high, will help you impact subsequent talks. The first number is going to be the starting point. Although you do not get the number, starting high, do lead to a higher offer from your employer.

Limit the availability

A psychologist has established one of the main concepts known as scarcity or restricting the supply of something. Research shows that when things are scarce or reduced, objects become more desirable.

People are more likely to purchase anything if they hear that it's the only one or that the deal will soon be over. An artist, for example, might only produce a small run of a single print. Because there are only a few prints left for sale, customers will be more likely to make a buy until they're gone.

Spend time notifying convincing communications

The examples above are only a handful of the numerous methods of convincing mentioned by social psychologists. Search for indications of persuasion in the day-to-day experience. A fascinating procedure is to watch a half-hour of random television shows and to remember any instance of convincing ads. You could be surprised by the sheer number of effective strategies used in such a short period.

How to detect emotions, deceit, and distress?

In your professional and personal life, you need to know who's a friend or an adversary and show you the truth or a bunch of lies. Various records may suggest whether people are excessively upset or nervous, which may be the product of their deception. However, only because you see a sign of deceit, the person might not be lying. There may be other situations at function, which is why it is important to resist generalization and try to search for signs of deceit in the proper sense. The more signals of deceit you see, the better the chances are that the individual is not real to you. Let's assume, for example, that you ask your buddy if he was at the bar last night and, in answer, he's rubbing his nose. The action might not be important on its own, but if it also blushes, stammers, swallows loudly, blinks a lot, and shuffles its legs, then you have ample proof that it hides something from you. If you learn all the signs of deceit and stress, you will become an extremely astute and effective human lie detector. If a person has cheated, the body responds, and there's a disagreement between what's wrong a guy doing and telling the facts.

What Breathing and skin alteration means?

Our ways of breathing change depending on the conditions, such as whether we're under severe stress or lying. You could observe people filling their lungs with the appropriate volume of oxygen and instantly releasing their breath. The explanation for this is that they are oxygenating their bodies when stress and fear have propelled their autonomic nervous system to work overtime. It takes a great deal of energy to fabricate and mislead. Every organ in the body — respiratory, skin, digestive, and neuromata — goes into high gear in reaction to elevated stress. You will even unexpectedly see people's faces blow out as they expel oxygen. This move, too, is the effort of their bodies to relieve the anxiety they accumulated during the discomfort of their deceit. When individuals get highly nervous, they undergo other changes, including altering the color and brightness of their skin. For example, in fair-skinned individuals, the color will shift from a soft shade of pink to a bright red to white and even a greyish brown. When their blood supply increases, their skin represents this transition. You may see a shift in color in those with light skin, but it is much harder to observe in darker-skinned individuals whose skin color can darken further or appear ashen (greyish).

In addition to seeing changes in the color of the skin, you can see sweat. When you see someone being dishonest, you can see tiny dots of sweat come out of the person's upper lip and then on his forehead, making it look shiny. As the sweat falls, you'll see her clean the sweat from her forehead and forehead, just another sign of deceit. The sweat also migrates to the palms of the hands, leaving them clammy if you shake their hands or brush their palms. Then you'll see them wash their dirty hands together or pull on their dress.

Shaking body

Shaking is also the reaction of the body to terror. In the case of a liar, it stems from the anxiety of being caught. When the body temperature of people who are under tension or lying is increasing, they can do what they can to relieve themselves of the pain of feeling hot, such as loosening their belt or placing their finger under their collar to loosen it. It is also not rare to see the skin broken out in red patches or bumps due to temperature variations. Stress and fear will make them swallow hard, so they feel like their throat muscles are contracting. There are unconscious behaviors that look like life-saving gestures to them, but which translate into warning signals of deceit for you.

As the flow of blood varies, the veins and capillaries expand. People experience pain in tiny capillaries in their bodies, like the sensitive mucous membranes around the nose. That's why to reduce their pain, and people would immediately start pulling on or scratching their nose, eyebrows, ears, or cheeks and around their mouths. Because of this itchy or awkward feeling, you can see their lips swing to the side, pinch together, or spread, which is a common sign of deceit when it comes to questioning.

Shaking of muscles

As muscle tension is considerable, it is not rare for muscles to contract and become weaker. As a consequence, the individual feels uneasiness or shakiness. You will also see that in their hands as they lift something like a cup of water. You can see it in their legs as their posture becomes relentless. Shaking is also the reaction of the body to terror. In the case of a liar, it results from the anxiety of being caught. The body undergoes a temperature shift as it learns that something scary or unpleasant is going to happen. So, a trembling or vibratory motion may be produced to better control the temperature rise due to anxiety. Most generally, someone who experiences nervous anxiety is deceived by shakiness in his or her voice. Vocal muscles, which are the size of a thumbnail, get strained, sparking vocal tremor, and the pitch breaks as the person talks.

What the eyes can reveal?

When people blink a lot, it's a protective reflex. For instance, if someone unexpectedly raised a fist and came to you, you'd instantly come back and start blinking. The response is nature's way to clear your eyes for clearer vision, so you're ready for what the other person may do to you. The same thing happens when you're nervous. You twitch a lot to protect yourself from someone who is challenging you about your misdeeds. This behavior can also indicate feelings of ambiguity or vulnerability. If people feel humiliated, embarrassed, or anxious, they will automatically look away from you. Some people find it impossible to keep eye contact, which is why, when you ask someone a question and lie in response, they're going to change their line of vision.

How people show self-soothing habits?
Feeling discomfort makes people anxious, and they want instant relief from these emotions, and they will naturally do actions that cause fun experiences. For example, they can rub one or both of their eyes, much as babies do when exhausted or angry. They can frequently stroke certain parts of their body, such as their forearm or thigh. They could scratch their heads, not because they're scratching, but because they feel fine. Initially, the body temperature increases during tension and

gradually goes into what is known as homeostatic equilibrium and starts to cool down. A depressed or lying person may begin to feel a rush of coolness in his body and start constantly rubbing his fingers or palms of his hands together to generate heat.

Similarly, as people indulge in self-sustaining actions, they can often threaten to harm or even mutilate themselves to escape them—the pains of their fear that will make them feel better. Some are self-mutilated and feel bad as a way of humiliating themselves. You may have seen people pick their palms and fingers until they bleed. More often, you see them pinching or twisting their skin, dragging their ears, chewing their lips, scraping their fingers or toes, scratching themselves violently, or even bashing their heads.

Eye contact is a prove to truth

It doesn't matter whether people turn their attention to the left or the right or up or down. The important point is they've changed their eyes. There is a line of thought and misconception perpetuated in several body language books that were looking up implies that people are visually-oriented and need to be referred to in visual words, such as "I see" or "Look at this," while looking to the right or the left implies that they are auditory people who can connect to words such as "I hear you" or "Listen to this." When somebody unexpectedly squints his eyes, and a furrowed line emerges in the center of his forehead when asking, it's typically a giant tale of deceit. Their eye expression shows that they're frustrated, irritated, or angry that you're asking questions. You can even see their forehead lines as they wide open their eyes, all of which reflect confusion at your probing awareness of their lie. Some people will avoid eye contact with you constantly to make you believe they're telling the truth. This is a big thing to say, and no one who is saying the truth is continually looking at you, whether he or she is blind.

The response of mouth and lips

The best thing to say about whether people lie or are under severe stress is that they have trouble lubricating the interior of their mouths. Their mucous membranes dry up, and they have trouble swallowing and forming phrases. Their tongue becomes stiff and starts to cling to the inside of their upper lip along with their teeth. That's why you see liars or people who are stressing out lick their lips and swallow them, pinch their lips, and even swing their lips in an unconscious effort to generate more saliva to ease their embarrassment. With little saliva in their mouth, the liars become thirsty, and it is not rare for them to put down a bottle of water in one sitting room. This is commonly done while a convicted suspect is being interviewed during a criminal inquiry.

Involuntary muscles action

The most common muscle twitches occur on the temples and jaw lines, particularly when the jaws clench together. This, too, is the autonomic nervous system that functions while someone is under threat. When you see someone's temples pulsating, they are mostly the product of elevated blood pressure and muscle strain. When the jaws clench tightly, this is also the product of muscle strain. Muscle tension is also prevalent in the spine, particularly in the back. It is not surprising, however, to see people frozen the back of their necks or put their hands there while they indulge in deceit. Another significant to say when a person lies is the shrug of the shoulder. That is how the body loses muscle stress that happens when a person formulates a lie or when they are confronted about non-truth. Liars can suddenly move or shuffle their feet if they ask a critical question or make a lie. It's their body's way of suggesting they want to run or leave the scene to get away from the interrogation.

Deliberately misleading talk

There are many sayings in a person's speech where that person is not real. Here are some of the things they're trying to do:

- Answer a question with your question.

- Send a roundabout answer or get off the tangent instead of sticking to the point while answering a question.
- Repeat the terms and phrases.
- Make psychodynamic slips in which they will confess wrongdoing and then quickly right themselves.
- Talk loudly to pretend confidence, particularly when challenged or confronted.
- Vocally perish after important words or sentences.
- Speak too much and offer too much knowledge that is not important.
- Pause and stammer about main topics, using a tone of "yeah" and "um."
- Stop for a long period during which they create their lie.
- Go on the protective and turn the tables.

- Talk in a trembling voice.
- They also clear their throats.

You can notice these people in your personal life, your business affairs, and even your family. They can be male or female, young or aged. To give you the Body Language Advantage over these toxic styles to quickly identify them and interact with them accordingly — by setting limits or not allowing them to join your life.

CHAPTER 8: BODY LANGUAGE MASTERY

Almost 93 percent of the conversation is non-verbal, indicating that it has nothing to do with language. When it comes to conversation, what you say doesn't even mean so much. It's more about how you say it. Yet non-verbal contact is not a conventional language. It is abstract, complicated, and often confounding. There are six keys to sharpen your non-verbal communication skills.

Get some encouragement

Learning the non-verbal language is not a challenge for the faint-hearted. You need to be inspired, and you just want to improve the ability to communicate non-verbally. There's nothing simple about it, of course. You're going to have to invest a lot of effort and energy into it. You will need to set goals, get guidance about your mistakes and achievements, and work.

Strengthen your body language for your reading skills

If you wish to practice non-verbal communication, the most important thing you can do is try to 'read' the non-verbal signals of other people. You need to be observant and attentive, and you need to be focused on getting through with this. You're going to want to get feedback and focus on consistency. That's why it's a smart idea to look for a coaching mentor who can help you climb the ladders and sharpen your skills.

Convey body language to others

This is the encoding, or more, the capacity to convey non-verbal information to other people through posture, facial expressions, movements, and tone of voice. Research suggests that non-verbal encoding and decoding abilities are related. If you're very good at decoding the body language of others, you'll note that you're still very good at conveying body language yourself. To make the best out of body language, you need to improve the capacity to communicate the emotions authentically and learn to be a strong emotional performance.

Remove micro-expressions

There are tiny gestures that can be very confusing. Micro gestures misrepresent your motives and can even ruin the picture you're trying to portray. You should learn to keep your face calm, rock-solid while you talk. Start by practicing with a mirror. Take a look at your reflection in the mirror, and start talking. Concentrate on some odd micro-expressions on your face when you're going through specific emotional states. Try to say the same thing again while keeping your face stable and strong. You should do this work out for about 15 minutes a day.

Understand ethical values

To send correct non-verbal communications, you need to grasp social norms. Of course, different signals can mean different things depending on the context of their use. To be a more effective communicator, you can consider the communication context. There is no way you can learn body language without knowing social conditions.

Non-verbal regulatory skills

You must be able to control your non-verbal actions based on social efficacy. You may have to hide your feelings sometimes. If your emotions are very strong, you won't be involved enough to consider the non-verbal interactions of others. Learning body language is not easy, but it can be achieved all the same. You're just going to have to do the training and be dedicated to learning.

Different ways constructive body language will make your life a better one

You possibly now know that constructive body language will have a significant influence on your life. Research explains that constructive body language will have a strong influence on everyone. Good body language refers to aspects like constructive listening, appropriate eye contact, and some targeted movements that can make someone more professional, likable, and convincing.

1. Change the behavior

Studies suggest that the implementation of constructive body language has a significant effect on the hormones. Research also explains that changing the body's vocabulary to make it meaningful strengthens the attitudes. This is a significant advantage, provided that a good outlook will make you more effective in addressing the problems of your career and your personal life.

2. Enhance the presence

By changing your body language to make it more optimistic, you will significantly enhance your image. You will give out stronger messages and alter the way people see you. Whenever you get a little down, you should still use power body language to get your life back. Trying to get up, stretch your chest, and keep your head straight for just two minutes. More often than not, you will note how much stronger and more secure you are. You will also have a strong effect on the people around you by practicing a constructive body language.

3. Tends to increase testosterone

Testosterone is an essential hormone in the body, whether you are a male or a woman. It's not just about sports, rivalry, and athletics. It boosts your confidence and makes you feel more secure and trustworthy around the board. Scientific tests have shown that positive body language will increase testosterone levels by up to 20%.

4. Prevent confrontation

Whenever we are irritated or frustrated, we use a particular body language. By mastering defensive body language, we can say it when the people we communicate with get offended. Just assume how many unpleasant experiences you would prevent in this manner. Improving your body language and having a clear perspective of the body language of others is a good way to stop the confrontation.

5. Talk better to people

Up to 93% of all human contact is non-verbal. By following a constructive body language, you will become a more effective communicator. This, in particular, will help you to interact with the people around you and broaden the scope in a professional context.

6. Decreases the stress hormone

Studies have found that positive body language reduces cortisol levels (a stress hormone that adversely influences output and induces detrimental health effects over time) by up to 25%. While using this hormone in your body, supportive body language will reduce discomfort and improve your performance in daily activities.

7. Improves emotional, intellectual ability

One of the core aspects of emotional intelligence is the ability to express thoughts and feelings accurately. People with negative body language have a damaging and spreading impact around them. By learning to strengthen your body language, you will increase your Emotional Intelligence and be a happier person around others. By taking a few minutes per day to develop your body's vocabulary, you will transform your life better.

Unusual facts about body language reading

Non-verbal communication is a social language that is stronger than our vocabulary will ever be. Non-verbal communication mastery will give you specific advantages in both your personal and corporate life. Perhaps this is why so many life skills coaches discuss the value of knowing body language. As you continue on your quest to learn body language, so that you can make your life a lot easier, it's crucial to keep the following body language details in mind.

It's not all black and white

What many body language specialists don't advise you is that everything is not black and white. Specific gestures have no specific significance. Rather, they're undefined. For, e.g., if anyone crosses their arms, this may be taken to indicate that they indicate defensiveness. But they might be freezing, too, or they might just want to get relaxed. If you strive to improve body language, keep in mind that movements can only be understood based on particular situations. There is no single law that applies to all of us.

Facial body language can be tricky to read

Most adults have perfected the art of masking their real emotions, rendering the face a poor place to start interpreting body language. People just like to get along at home, at work, and in diverse social environments. For that cause, they still appear to smile and believe that their faces are soft when they're genuinely pissed. Much of the time, the face is a friendly mask that veils our real emotions from the outside. Understanding this will come in handy when you continue to develop your body language reading skills. Even the face can carry away some of our deepest emotions, even if they are related to micro-expressions. These are all the unintended releases in our true feelings that break through the shield of the mind. Such micro-expressions can occur for a fraction of a second, and it will take you a lot of training (and practice) before you can understand how to pick them up.

Body language indicates the purpose

A general idea out there is that body language is a symbol of intent. Instead, body language conveys emotional meaning, with some pretty decent precision. Scientific experiments indicate that our emotions first reveal up in the body, before appearing in the conscious mind seconds later. If you are impatient, frustrated, satisfied, or starving, your body will reveal these emotions to a considerable extent. So, trying to master body language has more to do with learning to decode other people's behaviors, not their conscious thoughts.

Read the body language of the people you know

People can more easily tell when their partner is pissed or when their child is bored. You can also see when your employer wants you to do something. Because you've spent a lot of time around people in your close circles, you've gained a wealth of information about their body language cues. Also, the people we know well, though, can betray us.

Body movements hack to control frustration and other aggressive emotion

Emotions, both positive and negative, are helpful. These should be articulated acceptably. It exists, however, that a lot of people prefer to control frustration and other feelings to match what they believe is 'socially-approved' behavior. The theory is that by suppressing anger (or other negative emotions), you won't be seen as a 'cry baby.' The resulting embodiment of feelings is dangerous and sometimes leads to conflict between partners, difficulty sleeping, and a lack of confidence in the things you enjoyed doing.

Lookup

There is a persistent feedback loop of body language and emotions. Each of them appears to influence the other. The next time you feel like anger is getting the better of you, and you should use this to your benefit. There are few things worse than doing negative things because you're upset and apologize later when you didn't mean it. Looking up at the ceiling or the sky is a perfect way to use body language to unleash frustration. People appear to look down when they're in a negative condition.

Think of a kid who's been reported misbehaving. What's the body language? They're more likely to look down and avoid eye contact. This is one way the body communicates negative feelings. Looking down continues to give way to negative feelings. So, the next time you find yourself squarely trapped in the grips of rage, translate the negative body language and do the reverse (which is looking up). Essentially, you're going to disrupt the depressive feeling and cause pleasant hormones to be released.

Keep smiling

Did you know that having a smile or laughter can heal from aggression and other negative emotions? Laughter is a perfect way to improve your mental state. The next time you find yourself getting upset or having a really bad mood, think of something that made you laugh. You can display something funny on your computer, too. It's going to be tough to remain angry while you experience something that makes you smile or laugh.

Take a deep breath

Take a long breath away; anger and frustration continue to make our breathing shallow and quick as the body slips into its battle or flight reaction mode. You should deny this effect by deliberately altering the breathing patterns so that it's longer and stronger. This helps you get back to a state of mental balance while you calm down. When you breathe slowly, concentrate on lengthening the time of your exhalation. For, e.g., you should count to 4 as you breathe, and then ten as you empty your lungs when you're exhaling, pretending that you're blowing out your frustration into the breeze.

Write it down

Scientific evidence indicates that creative writing has therapeutic advantages. Any time you find yourself getting upset or feeling bad about something, write it in your diary. This tends to flush away negative feelings and can also shift your outlook. If you've finished writing your feelings, feel free to get a fire, and burn the page. Visualize all the rage (or some other emotion dragging you down) flying up in the smoke. All of these basic exercises will help to disrupt the depressive state so that you will feel awesome again. Bottling negative thoughts does more harm than good. Instead, work on releasing emotions that drag you down positively and productively.

How to use nonverbal communication to improve the mood?

Your body communicates to both the inner and outer environments. Your body language has a significant influence not only on how people view you but also on how you are. Poor posture affects your physical fitness, affects your emotional disposition, and tells others a nasty tale about yourself. Many of life's greatest players have used body language to convey thoughts, win debates, and get what they want. Body language to combat anxiety. Do you know that your facial expression could affect your mood? Scientists found that patients with depression could improve their situation by presenting fewer frown lines on their forehead. Your body language has a strong impact on your feelings. If you follow a body language of trust (good stance, power pose, etc.), you begin to feel more secure.

On the other hand, if you curl up (poor balance, slouching, etc.), you appear less confident and uncertain. You owe it to yourself to use constructive body language to improve your mood. Start by enhancing the stance and other supportive body language features.

Move and free up your mind

When people are extremely upset, we frequently suggest, "Take a stroll." Why? Because a simple walk will change the state of their minds. Data shows that when people walk comfortably (right back with easy, light steps), they appear to be happier. People who walk unhappily (heavy knees, dangling shoulders) become more aggressive. Your posture influences your emotional state and also determines whether you are likely to pay attention to positive or negative facts.

Force a smile to raise the mood

Try to force a smile or a joke (for long enough) the next time you find yourself down. You're going to be shocked to know that this is lifting your spirits (even if for a moment). You will make this work much easier by attempting to take a picture of something you find amusing (or make you laugh). It's a perfect way to disintegrate a negative feeling and improve your attitude.

Trying to dance to stay positive

Have you ever been with someone who's been trying to cheer you up? And you never knew how pervasive their passion was? It was the body language of communicating. Everything beautiful about a little dance (either you or someone dear to you) prevents a negative mood. But what if you're in an atmosphere where dancing is not appropriate? You could be working in the workplace where there are clients and wanting to change the attitude. Consider walking a few paces or jogging softly. It's going to have the same impact as a dance. Body language has a huge influence on how you think and how others perceive you. Invest a little time every day to check your body language to identify things that need change to concentrate on it.

So, friends, we hope you've had a fun and insightful reading about body language fundamentals and how to use them in business. Note, the trick is to learn body language in series, not in isolation. Only looking at the angled movement of the head, but missing the cynical tone might offer a false impression of honest conversation. Perhaps most critically, you have to realize that when you research the body language of others, some will be actively scrutinizing yours, too. Try to take some time from your routine to focus on your body language to avoid providing intimidating or offensive messages by your movements to expressions. However, you don't mean any damage. In short, body language is non-verbal communication consisting of kinesics (movement of the body), haptic (touching), and proxemics (distance). It's very present in our daily lives, as many signs of body language can already be seen in half an hour. The role of body language can be to communicate meaning, to manage the flow of information through the use of eye behavior, and to have the potential to influence others. Most notably, body language communicates the emotions/identity and can control our interactions through signals of attachment, the immediacy of action, and recognition of our feelings. Body language is an integral aspect of the communication process. It not only does facilitate verbal expression to be conveyed more easily, but it also provides a voice to express feeling and message. However, the sense of body language varies based on community, gender, or age, which makes it more complicated and confused. To use it effectively, people should understand

and develop their understanding to prevent this dilemma. Applying body language to regular contact is a wise and insightful way to get in touch with someone; let's do it and make sense of it. Language consists of spoken and non-verbal languages. Non-verbal-language, or body-language, plays an essential role in transmitting signals as people communicate with others. Data reveals that 7 percent of the overall effect of a message is verbal, 38% is oral, and the remainder is non-verbal (55%). Moreover, the main field of face-to-face communication, more than 65 percent, is non-verbal, while verbal is less than 35 percent. The influence of body language is important in everyday life. This book addresses what body language is, what particular impact it has on communication, and how to use body language effectively.

COPYRIGHT

A statement of principle is a subcommittee of the American Bar Association, a committee of publishers, and is approved. A copy, reproduction, or distribution of parts of this text, in electronic or written form, is not permitted.

The recording of this document is strictly prohibited. Any retention of this text is only with the written permission of the publisher and all liberties authorized.

The information provided here is correct and reliable, as any lack of attention or other means resulting from the misuse or use of the procedures or instructions contained therein is the total, and absolute obligation of the user addressed.

The author is not obliged, directly or indirectly, to assume civil liability for any restoration, damage, or loss resulting from the data collected here. The respective authors retain all copyrights not kept by the publisher.

The information contained herein is solely and universally available for information purposes. The data is presented without a warranty or promise of any kind.

The trademarks used are without approval, and the patent is issued without the trademark owner's permission or protection.

The logos and labels in this book are the property of the owners themselves and are not associated with this text.